The Ready Maker Handbook

Secrets of Making Software

A Ready Maker Book
From Ready Makers, Inc.

www.getready.io

Grateful acknowledgement to the Flickr Creative Commons
Community for the photographs in this book.
Photo credits by image available at: www.getready.io/credits

Design: Aura Flores, Héctor Moncada
Design Direction: Jonathan Slimak
Activity Recipes: Katy Auchter
Copy Editor: Catherine Traffis
Author Photo: Hillary Raphael

Ready Maker Books
ISBN-13: 978-0998196503
ISBN-10: 0998196509
LCCN: 2016916436

Library of Congress Control Number: 2016916436
Ready Makers, Inc., New York, NY

For all the makers out there– this book is for you.

CONTENTS

I. INTRODUCTION

You're holding the key to Ready. It unlocks the secrets of a place as big — or small — as your imagination.

You're holding the key to Ready. It unlocks the secrets of a place as big — or small — as your imagination. Make a game, a world, a story — whatever you want. Then show what you've made, or keep it for yourself.

Along the way, you'll learn powerful concepts that control all computers. Things like conditional statements, cloning, classes, memory, physics engines, and much more. Normally, it takes years to learn these ideas, typically after you've mastered a computer language, like C or Javascript.

With Ready, you'll build your own software and experience these ideas without learning a computer language. You'll be initiated into a world that, until now, only computer programmers have been permitted to experience. And if you decide one day to learn computer programming, the odds are you'll be a lot better at it because you'll already know many of the advanced concepts well ahead of learning the syntax of a computer language.

At Ready, we believe everyone should be able to make software, and that you shouldn't have to learn a computer language to create the digital stuff we all use. So we built Ready to let you create what's in your head.

Some people told us not to bother — that it was impossible, stupid, too hard, or all of these mashed up in one big "NO." But we're futurists who believe we all get to make the future, together. When people say, "It can't be done," we don't think that it can't be done! So we made Ready anyway.

WE'RE READY

Are you?
Good! Turn the page.

GETTING READY

Ready runs on PCs, Macs, Android, and Apple iOS. You can pick your flavor and download Ready from: getready.io/download

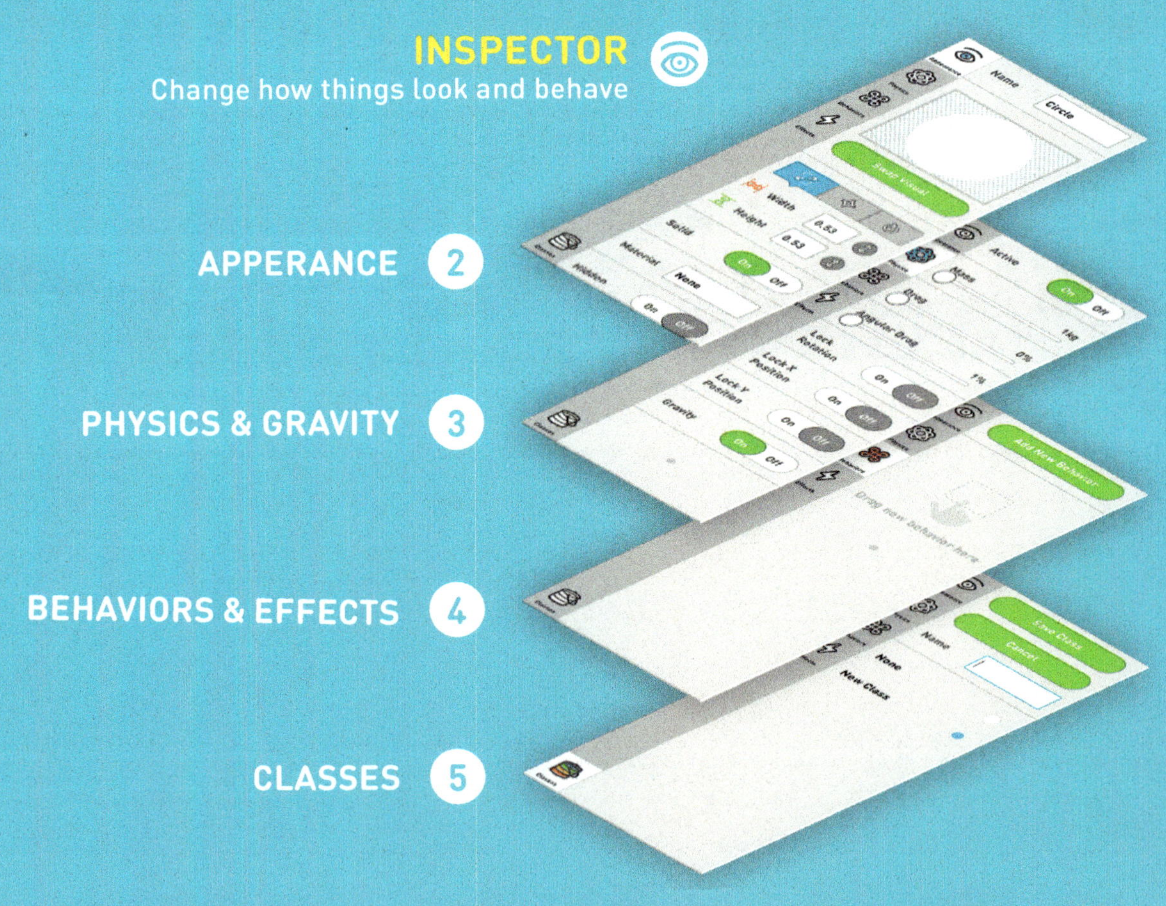

EVENT MANAGER
Give things instructions
1 CANVAS
LIBRARY
Add things to your project
6 BEHAVIORS & EFFECTS
7 INTERFACE & GAME
8 BACKGROUNDS
9 ARTWORK & BASIC SHAPES

II. DISCOVERING THE READY WORLD

All computer programming is like learning a language. You need some way to tell computers what to do. With Ready, we made a language that's easy to understand.

SPEAKING READY

In Ready we use words like these:

Projects: What you make and save in Ready.
Scene: What's inside the project, like a scene in a movie.
Objects: Things you put into your scene, like characters or vehicles.
Library: A place that contains many objects you can chose from.
Categories: Groups of objects. "Vehicles" contains cars, boats, and bicycles.
Backgrounds: Objects that serve as backgrounds to your scene, like grass or outer space.
Play / Stop: I bet you can figure out what this means on your own.

AUSTRALIA
1/2 tsp

In the beginning, an object is just a picture of a thing. Drag a picture of a ball onto your scene and it won't behave like a ball should. It won't bounce. Telling objects to do stuff is fun and exciting.

To make a ball "smart" it needs to acquire a behavior. Behaviors are like little bits of DNA that turn an otherwise inanimate object into a creature that has some capability. Once an object has a behavior, it's a smart object.

Ready uses recipes as a way of explaining how to build a project.

Making software is like cooking. When you learn to cook a dish, you follow a recipe, like a chocolate cake recipe, for example. That recipe tells you what ingredients you need (flour, sugar, chocolate), how to mix them together (this much water with that much flour), and then you put the mixture into the oven (time, temperature). At the end, you have a cake! Software is very similar. And as with cooking, once you've learned to make a dish, you can tweak it to make it your own style, and maybe invent something, like an upside-down chocolate cake.

Let's try making a smart object together.

To get this done, we are going to need to learn some new parts of the Ready language:

Behaviors: programmatic functions that teach an object to do something.
Physics: a special behavior that gives an object a sense of existing in a physical world, with weight and friction.
Event Manager: the place where we teach objects to interact with each other — and you!

EXPERIMENT!

TWO BUDDIES

As with cooking, we can begin by just describing the dish: Let's have two buddies on screen, where one always looks at the other, wherever it may go.

Here's the recipe to make this scene:

1. Drag two objects from the library onto the scene.
2. Tap the first object and give it a drag behavior.
3. In the behavior, turn on physics.
4. Press play. You can drag the object around the screen.

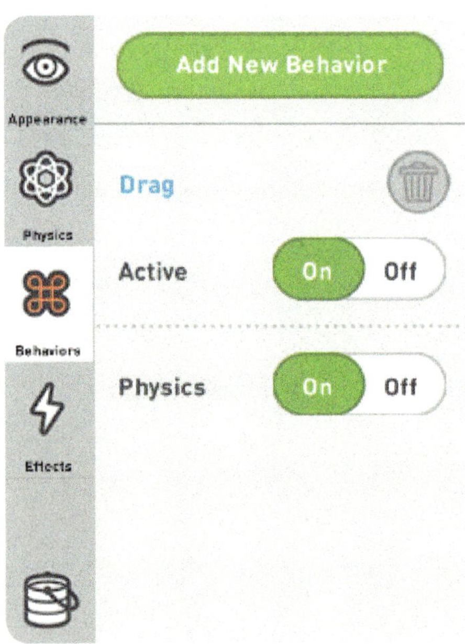

Let's do a little program to teach the second object to always look at the one being dragged.

1. Open the Event Manager. Write a sentence... WHEN first object's / drag / is dragging DO second object's / angle / face object / first object.
2. Press play. You should see the second object is always turning to face the first one.
3. Flick the first one... hard! Bye-bye!
Good! From now on, we will be using pseudocode as much as possible to describe programming events.

Ready is an infinite canvas and your screen is just a viewport on the scene. So the first buddy will continue to fly off, forever — or for as far as the memory of your device can contain.

Let's explore the Event Manager a bit more. You may have noticed that when you flick the first object, the second object stops turning toward it. Why is that? Look at what you wrote so we can use pseudocode to describe it. You said, "When the object is being dragged, Do turn angle to face it." But when it's flicked, you're no longer dragging it. So what's another way to tell the second object to always face the first?

Maybe we could say in pseudocode: "When the first object is sensing that it's being seen, the second object's angle should turn to face it."

Go ahead and try to program that on your own. Hint: the Event Manager is contextual. So you can back up to the tile that says Drag and tap it. From there you'll see another option such as Sensing. Tap the other option.

PHYSICS

Let's explore this world a little more.

1. Turn off physics from the first object's drag behavior.
2. Play and flick it. See how differently it moves? When physics are on, the object lives in a world defined by space, time, and motion. Just like our universe.
3. Turn physics back on in the drag behavior.
4. And turn on the main physics– the button above behaviors.
5. Press play. Uh-oh! Right away the object falls out of your scene!
6. Open the physics panel and this time turn gravity off. Play.

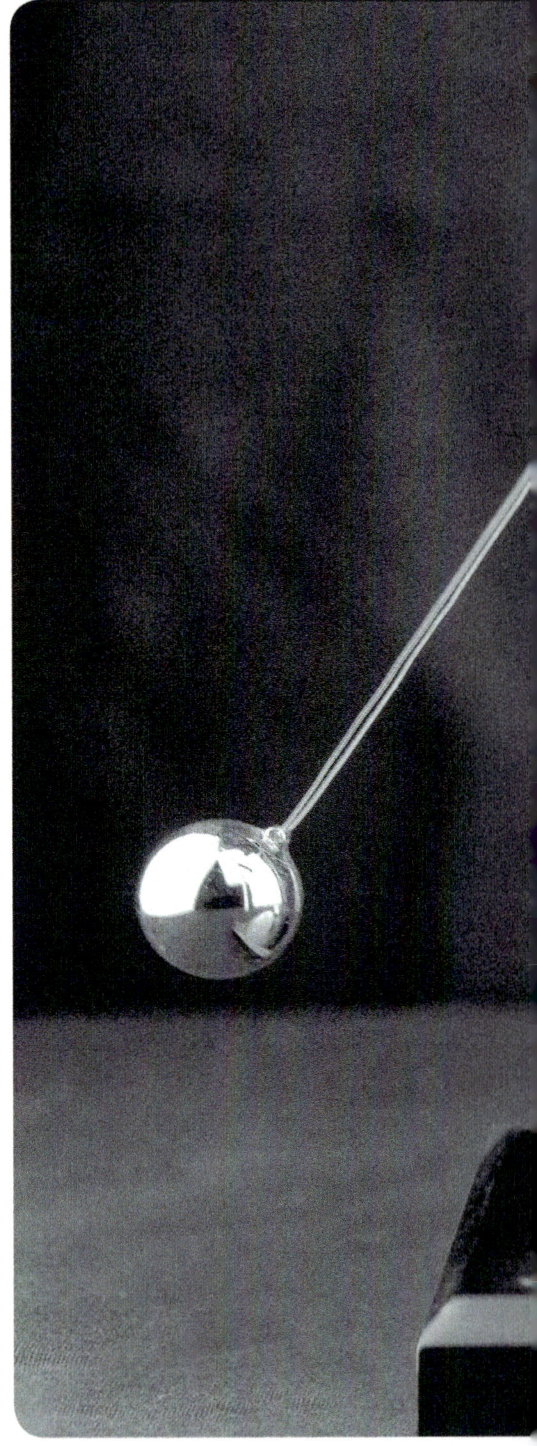

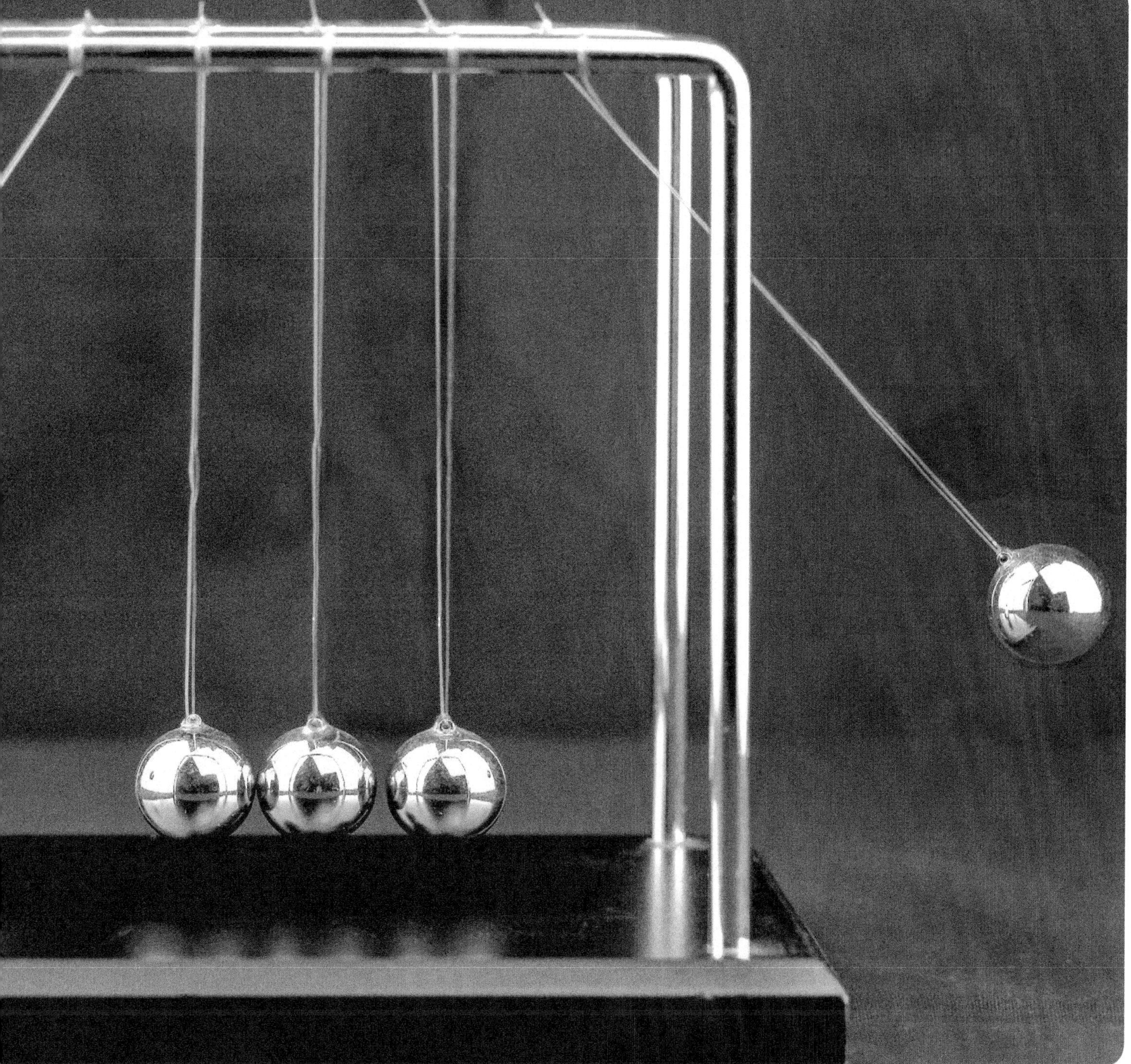

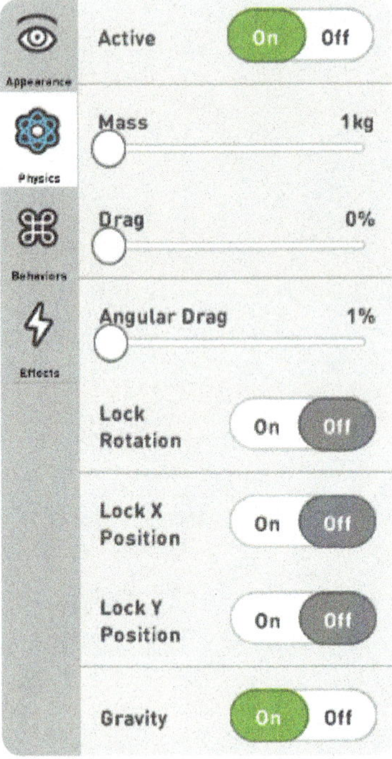

From here you can change the first object's mass in kilograms (2.2 pounds to a kilo) and drag. Think of drag like the creation of air or water. Without drag, the object moves through a vacuum, like outer space. A little drag — like 5% — and it's as if the object were moving through air. More drag and it's like a liquid, or a near solid at 100%, like heavy syrup.

Have fun playing with the physics settings and feeling how your scene changes. This is called tuning your scene, and it's what professional game designers do all the time — they tune the physics in their games to make them realistic, or to balance between easy and hard challenges.

STAY IN FRAME

Let's make the object stay inside the viewport, by using another behavior called Stay in Frame. Go ahead and add that behavior to the first object. You'll see a number of options, most importantly, reaction. This describes what Ready should do when the object leaves the viewport. Should it "wrap around" to the other side?

Go ahead and play with the options and see how they're different. Try changing the padding as well.

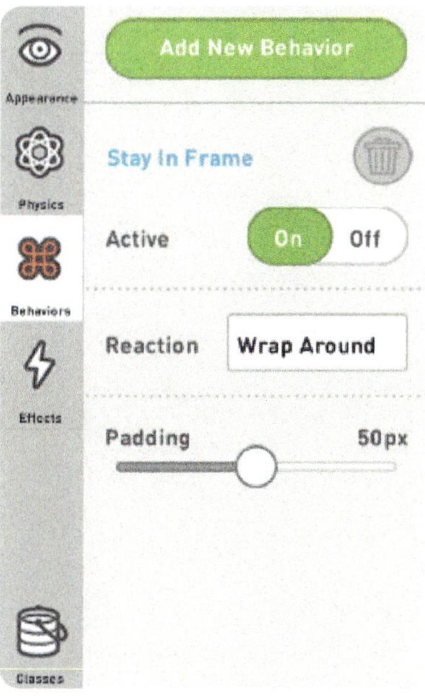

APPEARANCE

Objects have an appearance. Under appearance, you can change what the object looks like and what it's made of, tint it a different color, and more.

1. Go ahead and tint the object a different color.
2. You can also change its material. Make it bouncy and then flick it against the second object. Does it behave differently?
3. Try other materials, like wood. These change the object's elasticity. Wood is a lot less elastic than rubber. Drop a piece of wood on the floor. It behaves differently than a piece of rubber that weighs the same.

1. Let's customize our scene a bit. You can give the first object an effect. These are sensory properties the object can acquire. Give it a trail effect. Press play to see a trail develop when the object is dragged.
2. Go ahead and play with the different trail settings.
3. Add a background from the library... whoa! How quickly the scene changes!

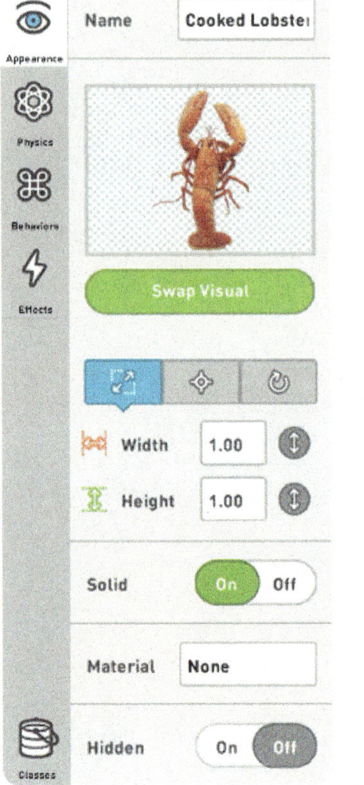

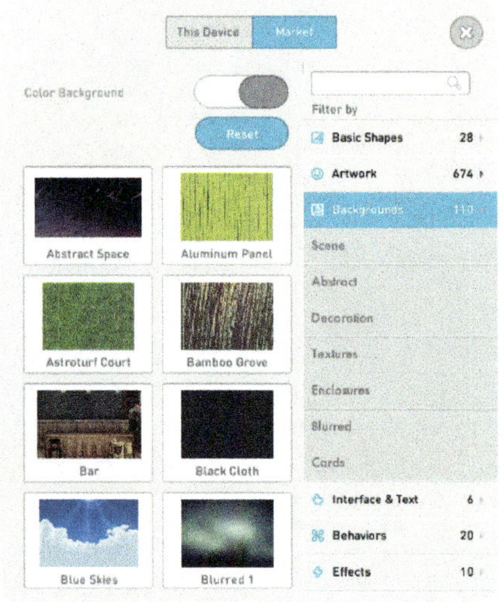

You can always tint the background, or remove it by toggling reset at the top of the list.

Your second object is always looking at the first. But maybe you want to change what the second object looks like, without affecting the code or behaviors?

Tap appearance and swap visual.
Find a different image, and drag it over. The second object will now look like that. You can repeat this as often as you want.

CLONING

Let's learn another concept, called cloning. Cloning is like the scene in Fantasia, when Mickey Mouse generates many broomsticks to do his job of carrying water. Let's give it a try.

1. Open the Event Manager and add a new event. Let's say that, "When the first object senses it's collided with the second object, do the second object clones the first object."
2. Give it a try and press play.

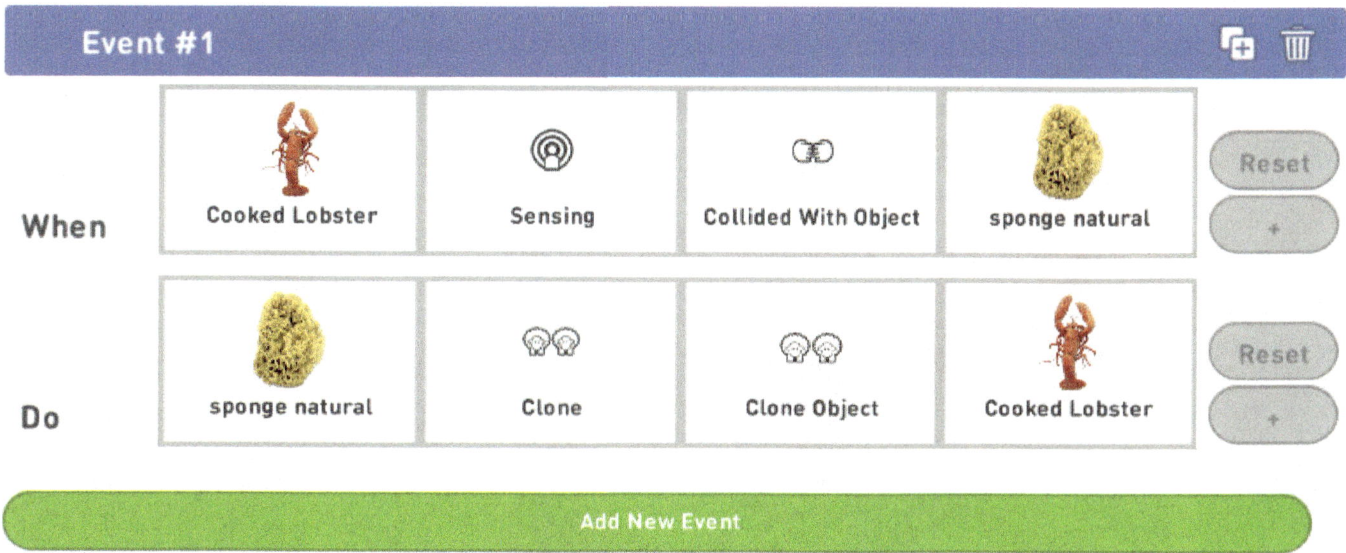

00

Whoa! You're duplicating objects!

You might notice a few things: Every clone is like the first one; it should be draggable and stay in the frame. But perhaps you noticed that the clones don't clone. Only the first one clones. You're learning a new concept: parent and child.

The first object is the parent, and the clones are children. If you want the clones to clone as well, then we have to put the parents and children into a family. In Ready, we call that a class. This is an advanced concept in computer science, but in Ready it's something you get to explore now!

CLASSES

1. Tap the first object and at the bottom left you'll see a paint bucket called classes.
2. Select it and then create a new class. You can call it "family" or anything else. Save it.
3. Go back to the Event Manager and let's change our cloning instruction to read, "When any object in the family class senses it collided with the second object, do second object clone first object."

Give it a try!

Many more clones appear. So many appear that you may notice the scene is running slowly and in a jagged fashion. Time to learn memory management and colliders.

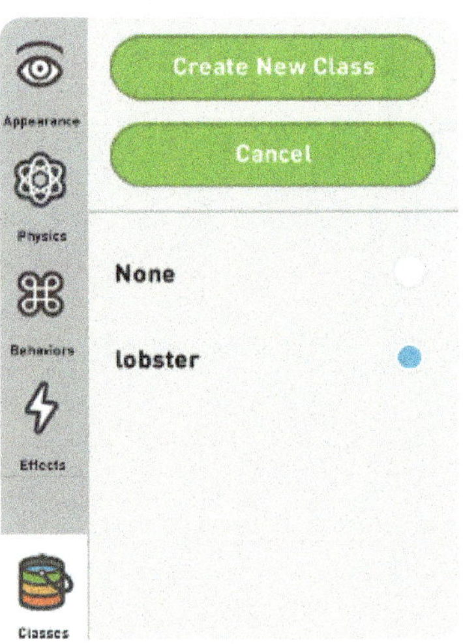

MIND BENDER

Can you clone forever? To infinity and beyond? Or will the computer eventually give up and crash? In Ready, clones are arbitrarily limited to 200 at a time. But there's a way to continuously remove clones and allow more to be made. Hint: "When any clone's existed for more than five seconds, do remove affected clone."

COLLIDERS

All objects have a collider around them. The collider is an invisible shape that surrounds the object. It's the shape the computer uses to sense where the object is, and whether it's hitting another object. In Ready, under appearance, you'll see an option at the bottom called collider. It's set by default to polygon. That means a shape is perfectly drawn around the object, like a glove around a hand.

Drawing perfectly shaped colliders is computationally expensive. It's fine when there's a small number of objects in the scene, but when there's a lot of them, the computer struggles to do all the math, calculating exactly what each object's collider might be sensing. In our scene, each clone also inherits a polygon collider.

1. Open Appearance for the first object.
2. Change the collider to be box or circle.
3. Play the scene. Should be smooth!

This is the kind of tradeoff professional programmers regularly consider: Do I give up precision for speed? Oftentimes, the right answer is determined by how this affects the user experience. In this case, the precision of a polygon collider has minimal benefit in the scene, while rapid and smooth cloning quickly improves the experience. So it's an easy tradeoff to sacrifice some precision to gain speed.

CONGRATULATIONS!

Take a breath for a minute, and appreciate all that you've learned already:

- Managing an infinite canvas, by using a stay in frame behavior.
- Activating a physics engine, and tuning it in a scene.
- Giving objects functional behaviors.
- Conditional statements: "When something happens, do something."
- Cloning.
- Inheritance in cloning.
- Parent and child distinctions between clones.
- Classes of objects.
- Colliders.
- Optimizing the user experience through memory management.

WOW!

Go ahead and save your project by tapping on the gear icon. You can set a project cover, giving it a name, and a description. Be sure to first save your cover, then save your overall project. Exit out of the scene. You should see the project in your workshop.

You're ready to level up.

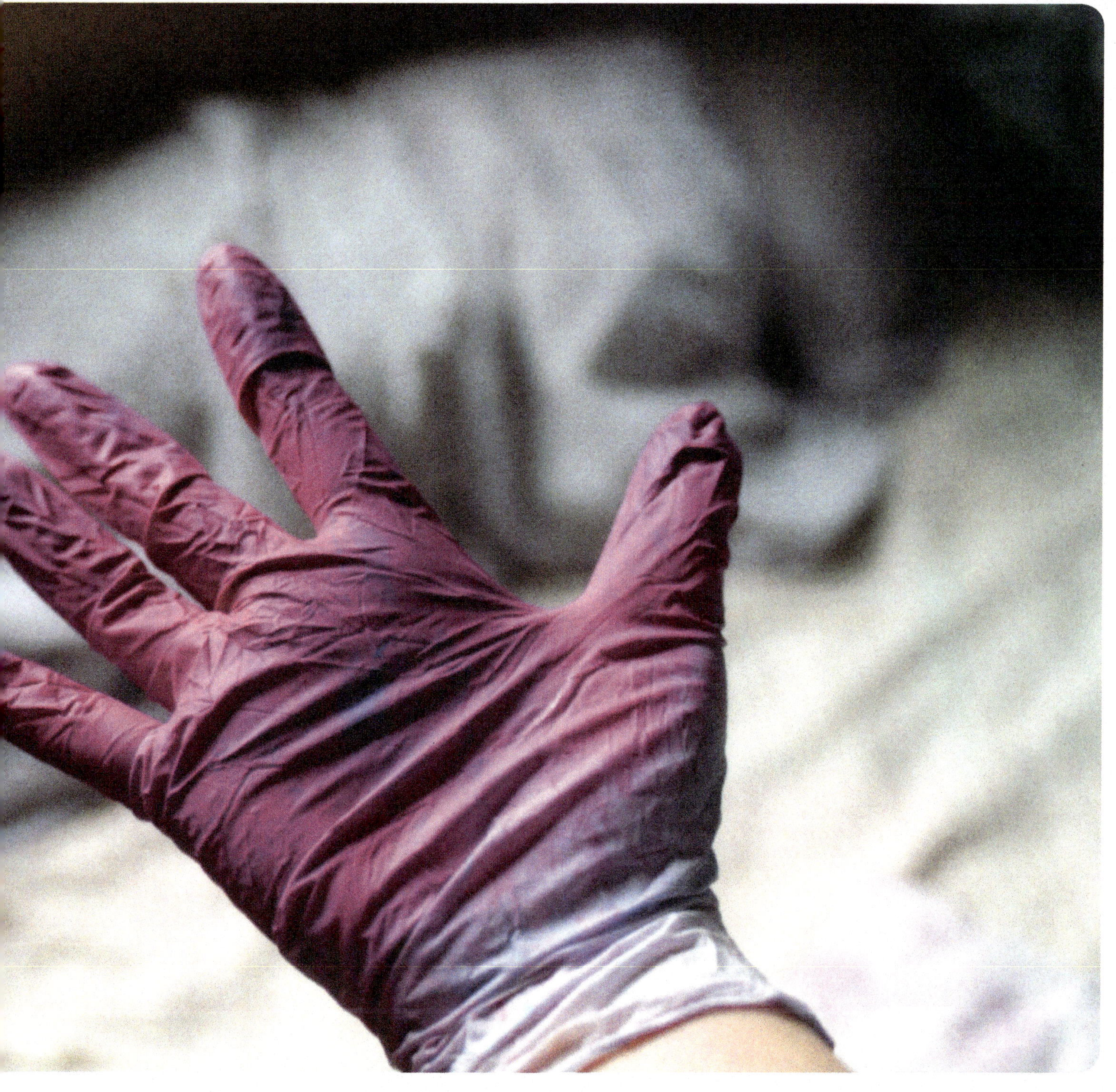

III. SPACE, TIME & MOTION: LIVING IN THE READY WORLD

Software exists in a virtual world. With a powerful enough computer, that world can be as big as our own.

CANVAS

Take a look at a blank scene. Notice the gridlines.
1. Tap twice on the screen and they'll disappear.
2. Tap twice and they're back. What are these gridlines? They look a bit like graph paper.
3. Tap the zoom out icon on the bottom, and the gridlines shrink down.

The gridlines provide a sense of scale. Each box is exactly 1 meter long and 1 meter tall. When you drop an object onto the scene, it has an actual size, measured in meters. Go ahead and explore.

1. Under appearance, you'll see width and height. This is a relative size; all objects start out as 1 high and 1 across.
2. Stretching the object, or squeezing the object will change its size.
3. Zooming out will make it appear smaller, but it won't change it's actual size. It's just moving an imaginary camera back in space. Each click takes you farther "away" from the scene, by a certain percentage.

CAMERA

Did you know that all software has a hidden camera, like in a movie? Ready exposes the camera to you. Let's play with the camera, and explore space.

1. Have one object in your scene.
2. Go into the Event Manager and write: "When the object is sensing touch down, do camera's position zoom out."
3. Tap on the object. Interesting! Every time you click, the camera moves away. Try clicking for as long as you can.
4. Here's a trick... make a tiny change to your code so that the camera keeps zooming out anyway by changing the when part to say, "When object is seen, do zoom out." It starts to feel like a movie! You'll notice there's a limit to how far out the camera will go — that's an arbitrary constraint in Ready. Maybe one day we'll let it zoom out forever!

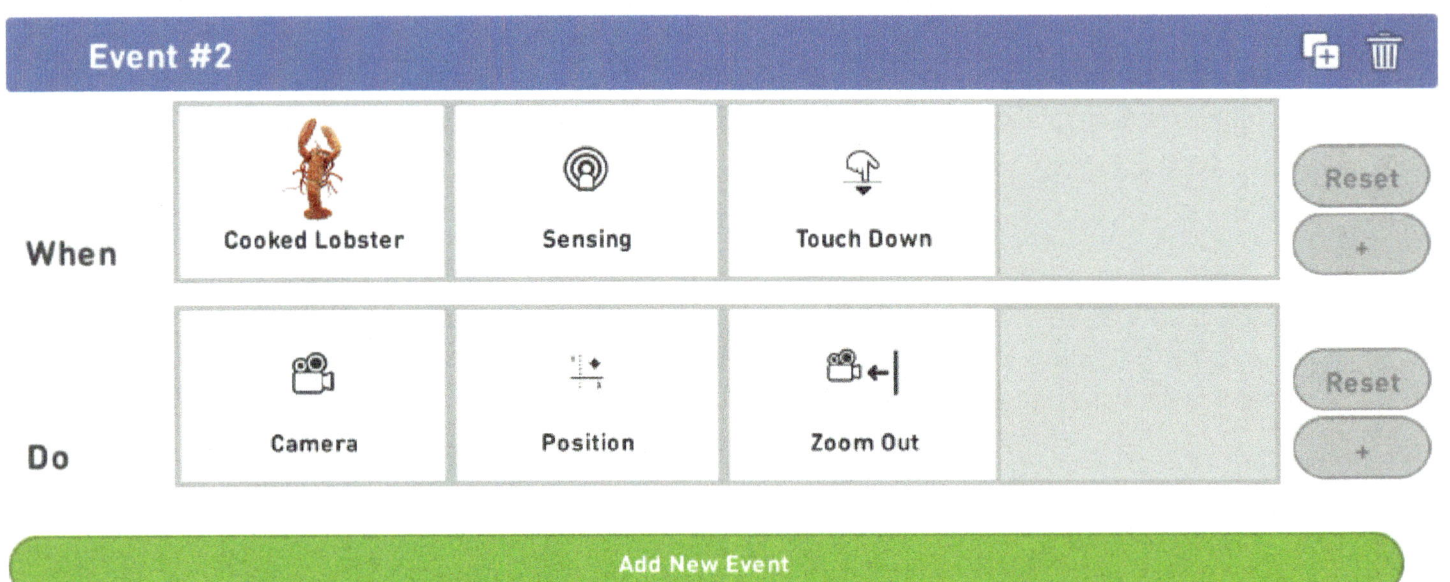

TURN TO CLEAR VISION
QUARTERS ONLY
50¢
INC.
TO OPERATE
TURN
HANDLE
ONE

Cameras can do lots of things in Ready. They can follow objects, which is how you can create levels in Ready. Build a scene inside the viewport. Zoom out and pan away. Then zoom back into empty space, and build a second scene. The camera can be programmed to go between these two scenes. So now you can have a start scene, a first level, a win moment, and a lose moment. Zoomed out on all your scenes, Ready looks like a secret map of the world you've made. Normally a user — that's the person playing your project —would never see the full map. Part of the fun is exploring the world, not knowing exactly how big it is.

1. In the Event Manager, there are controls that let you change the size of an object.
2. Create an event that says, "When the object is sensing touch down, do object's size grow 20." Now it feels like you're zooming in, but really, the object is growing by 20% on each tap. This is a good way to explore another aspect of space, which is sensing what's around you.
3. Change the command to be sensing touch held. Now tap and hold the object. See the difference?

MIND BENDER

Can you really zoom out forever? To infinity and beyond? Or will the computer eventually give up and crash? This is like asking, "Is the universe infinite?" It turns out the universe isn't infinite. It's 46 billion light-years across, and growing. Of course, we don't know what's on the other side! Is there another side?

Canon
CANON INC.
Φ58mm
1:3.5-5.6 II
CANON ZOOM LENS EF-S 18-55mm

MIND BENDER

Cartesian coordinates are a way of mapping the entire world. The Earth is mapped this way, through longitude (x-axis) and latitude (y-axis). Rene Descartes, a French mathematician, invented this system in the sixteenth century. It made exploring the world much easier, since navigators could now pinpoint an exact location, anywhere on Earth! In Ready, you're also an explorer, navigating a new world of your invention.

LAYERS

Let's learn about layers.

Even though the Ready world looks flat, like a piece of paper, you may have already got the sense that it exists in three dimensions. The two obvious dimensions are:

Up-down.
Left-right.

Ready thinks of space in geometric terms. Up-down is the y-axis. Left-right is the y-axis.

The x and y axes are like imaginary rulers, with increments measured in meters. The center of the universe is where the two rulers cross each other.

These two rulers let us give each object an address, or position on screen. The address has a specific rule: left-right position, and up-down position. This is written as (x, y). So (0,0) means the x position = 0, and the y position = 0. That places the object at the intersection of the two rulers.

These are called cartesian coordinates.

POSITION

At any time, you can inspect an object on screen and reveal its position.

1. Select an object and open Appearance.

2. Select the crosshair icon. Now you see the object's position on the screen.

Let's program an event to explore position.

1. When object sensing touch held, do set position (1,1).

2. When object sensing touch up, do set position (0,0).

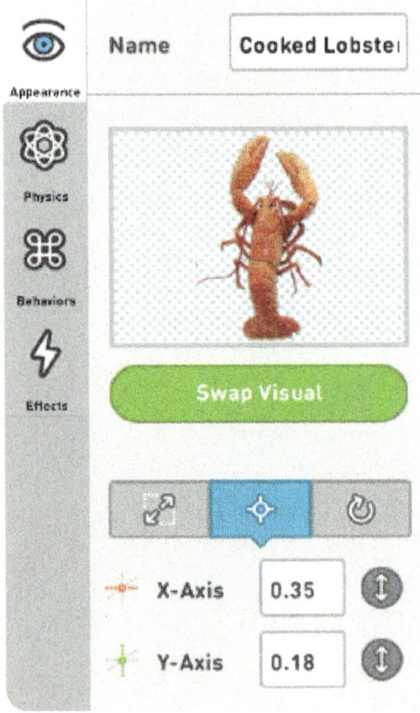

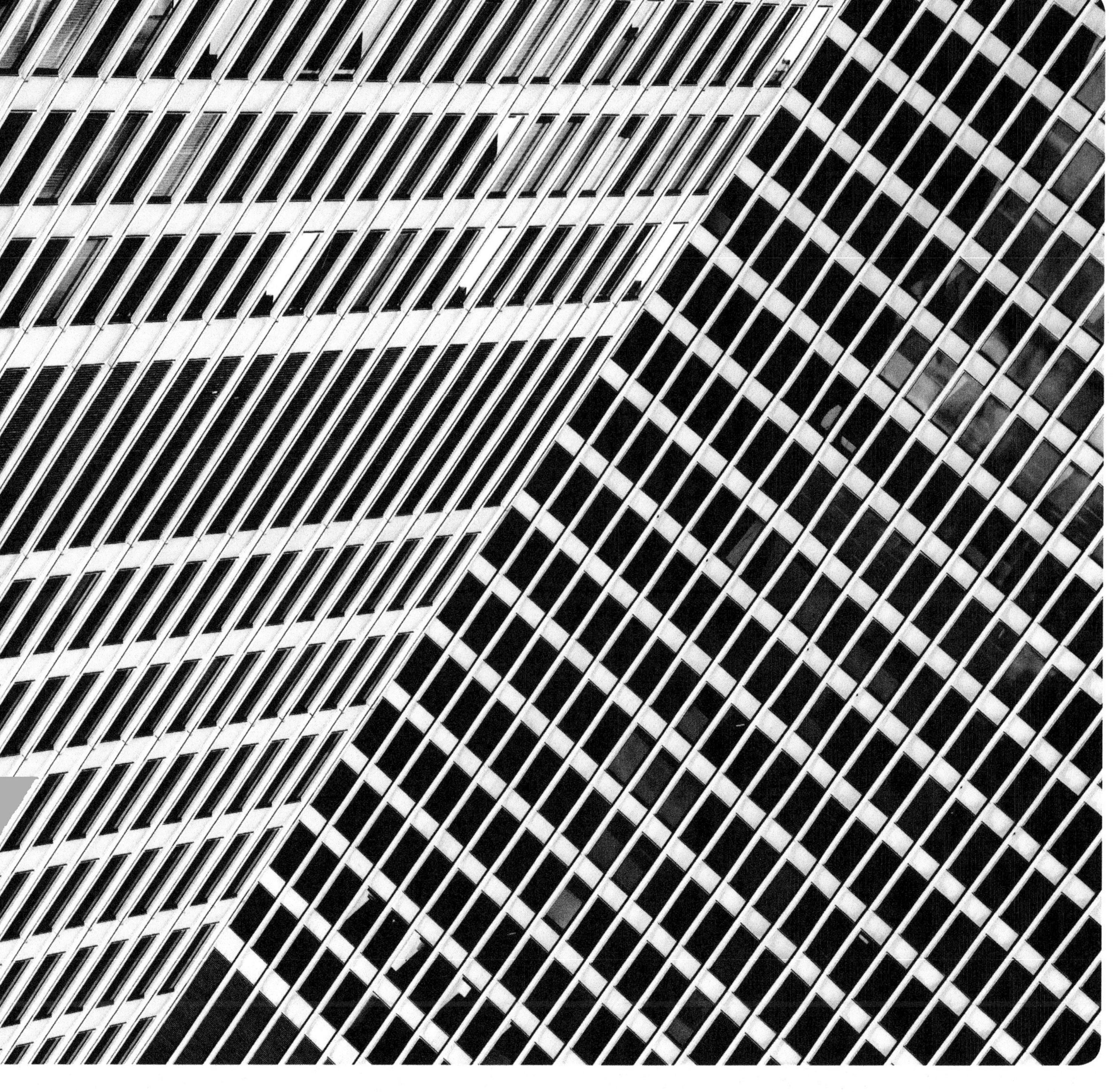

When you play the scene, the object will move up and to the right whenever you tap and hold down. Upon release, it returns to the center of the screen. Of course cartesian geometry allows for a third dimension.

In Ready, the third dimension is... **nearer-farther**.

Can you guess what letter that gets? The z-axis describes how close or far away the object is from the intersection of the x and y rulers. There's no way to actually put a third dimension on a flat plane, so it's illustrated like an imaginary see-through cube:The bigger the number is, the closer the object is to you. The full three-dimensional address is expressed as (x, y, z). So, (0,0,-1) is farther back, or "zoomed out." (0,0,0) is nearer, or "zoomed in." In Ready, z = 0 is as "near" to you as an object can be. There's no limit to how far back they can go.

Let's take a look.

1. Put an object on the scene.
2. Put another object on the scene and drag it over the first.
3. Notice how the second object is on top of the first object?
4. Select the second object and press the tiny farther-arrow. The second object will go behind the first object.
5. Press the nearer-arrow. The object moves on top of the other object.

What's really happening here is that the object is being sent either closer to you or farther away along a third dimension – the nearer-farther dimension.

TIME

What about 4D?
I'm glad you asked! Ready has a fourth dimension. Yep. It really does! Can you guess what the fourth dimension is?

The fourth dimension is time! Think of it this way: Imagine an airplane. Its altitude is the z-axis. The x and y coordinates are the spot on the Earth that the object is over. This describes a still airplane. Now... let's fly the plane. The velocity of the plane is the fourth dimension. Velocity describes the rate of change over time, or motion of the plane through space — how fast it speeds up or slows down. Congratulations! Putting these things together is called calculus.

Ready is a giant calculus engine that makes cool things happen. When you build things in Ready, you're generating very complex algebraic equations that tell the computer how to control the imaginary world you've made.

Our universe is made of three basic concepts: space, time, and motion. Each is defined as the product of the other two. Much of algebra and calculus is occupied by describing the combination of these things through numbers.

In Ready, time is expressed in two ways:
1. **Timers** that count in seconds.
2. **Frames** that count the redrawing of scenes.

What is "time"?
Time is motion over space. A mechanical clock uses the motion of a spring, releasing energy, to push a dial through space. When that dial passes a certain marker, we say a second or minute has gone by. All of time is movement. So, in a frozen world, which some people think is how the universe will end, time stops, because nothing moves anymore.

What is "space"?
Space is motion over time. For example a "light-year" describes the volume of space that light travels in one year. What is a meter? A meter is the distance light travels in about 3 nanoseconds. An interesting question: In a truly frozen universe where nothing moves any more, is there any space? If space is defined by motion over time, then this frozen universe could be measured as infinitely small... so the end is an infinitely tiny frozen universe that contains everything we've ever imagined.

What is "motion"?
Motion is space over time. If in one second I can move one meter, then my motion is described as "1 meter per second." I have traveled that much space (the meter) in that much time (a second). People say nothing can move through space faster than light, which travels 186,000 miles per second. Then again, maybe that's wrong.

Mind Bender: Quantum physics creates models of the universe that describe a particle called a quark, which may move faster than the speed of light, so fast that it's "instant." Meaning, the quarks can move from one place to another in zero seconds. Human brains are designed to live in three dimensions of space, plus the fourth dimension of time. So it's pretty hard for us to understand how this can work. Computers, on the other hand, can model as many dimensions as we want. So we use them to help us figure out these hard ideas.

TIMER

Let's see what we can do with a timer.

1. Under Interface & Text, find an object called timer.
2. Drag it to the screen.
3. Play.

The timer will count the passing of time in milliseconds. You can place as many timers as you like on the scene, and program against them.

1. Let's add another object to the scene. This object will control the timer.
2. Say, "When the object sensing touch down, do timer's timer label toggle timer."
3. Play the scene and tap the object.
4. Change the timer's appearance to be inactive at start. See the difference.

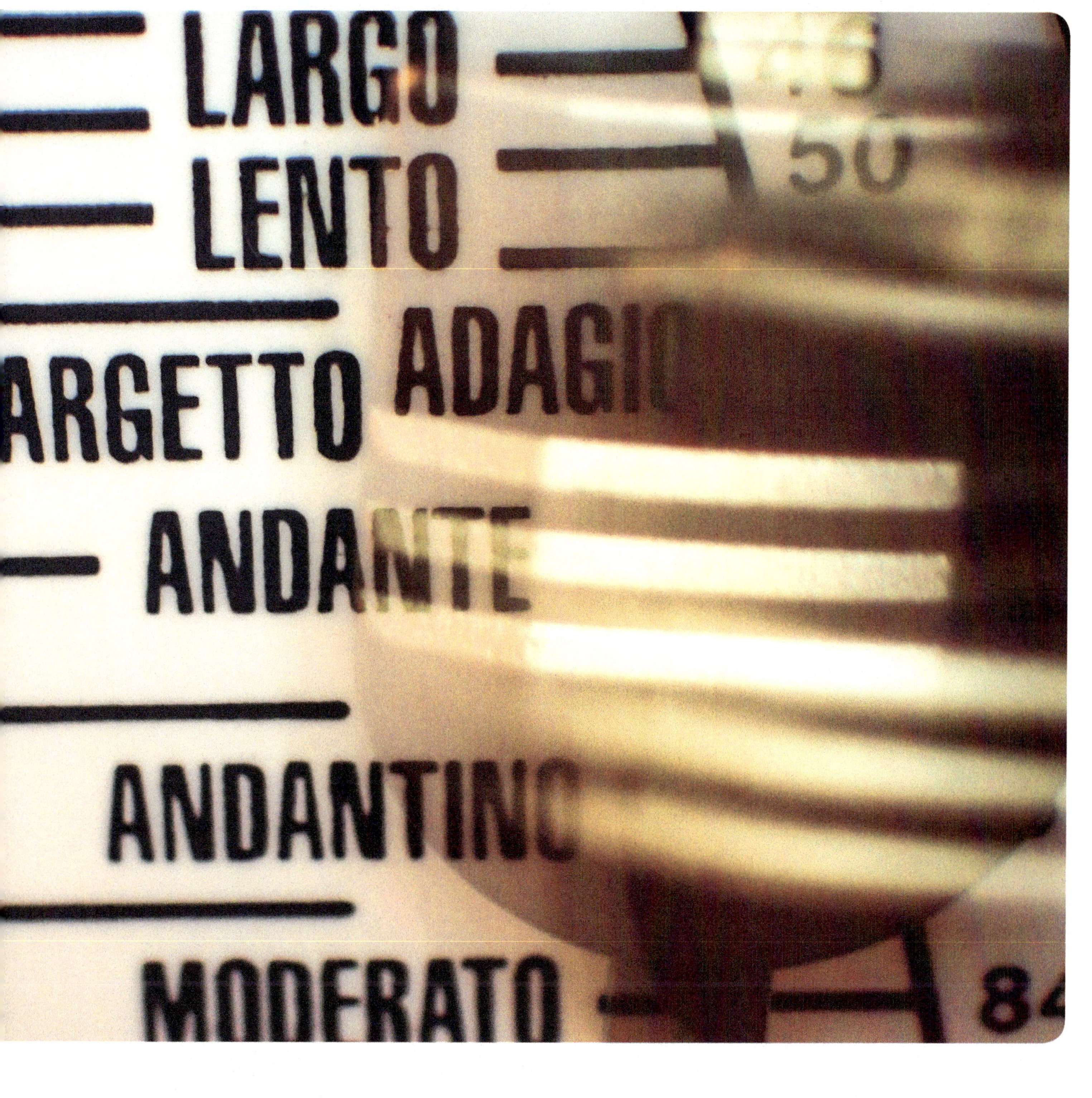
LARGO
50
LENTO
ARGETTO
ADAGI
ANDANTE
ANDANTIN
MODERATO
84

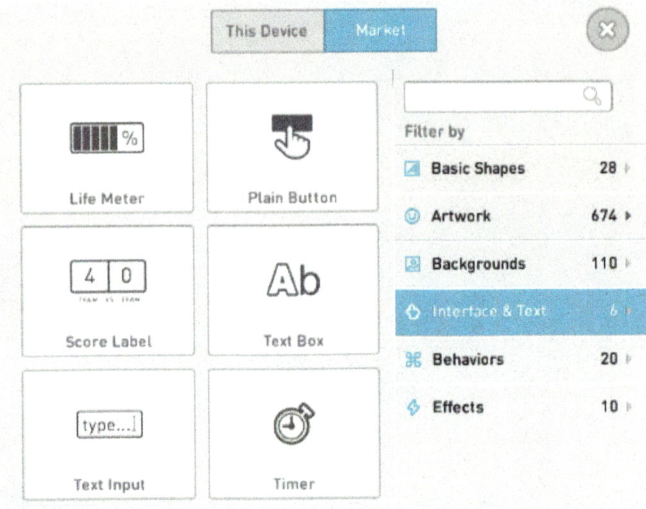

Each time you click the object, the timer will change state: If it's active, it'll stop; if it's stopped, it'll re-activate.

In a maze game, you might say a person has 60 seconds to get to the end, or lose. In a survival game, the challenge is living for as long as you can.

Another way of sensing the passage of time in Ready is through frames. A movie, for example, is an illusion created by showing 24 pictures per second. The human brain puts these still images together to see a "moving image." Ready operates the same way. Every second, Ready redraws the scene multiple times, to give the illusion of movement. Each redraw is a frame.

SYSTEM FRAMES

Frames can only be accessed in the Event Manager. They're a subset of the system object.

1. Add an object to your scene.

2. Say, "When system runtime every frame, do object play sound laser."

You'll hear a continuous sound each time you play your scene. That's because on every frame, the object makes that sound. The frames go by so fast that to our ears, the sound merges into a continuous wave.

The system object also comes with built-in timers of its own.

1. This time, change the command to say, "When system runtime repeat every 1, object play sound laser."

2. Now the system will command the scene to make a sound every second, for as long as the scene is running. **This is called runtime.**

Runtime is a program's master clock. All programs have an idea of runtime. Runtime can be thought of as a global timer, like the master clock measuring the age of our universe since the Big Bang.

A timer put on screen is a local timer measuring time independent of the global timer. Local timers can be stopped, started, and reset. But the global timer only stops when the scene ends. Kind of like the universal timer counting how long our universe has been around since inception.

MIND BENDER

In 1915, Albert Einstein proposed that the universe is full of local timers. This idea is called The General Theory of Relativity. Timers moving closer to the speed of light will seem to move much slower, relative to timers moving at a small fraction of the speed of light. In Ready, by starting and stopping local timers, and running them at different speeds, you can mimic the effect that Einstein imagined. But you can't affect the overall runtime speed. That's unchangeable.

VELOCITY

The Ready universe describes motion through physics. This is how scientists explain reality as well. Physics is the study of how energy and matter work together to create our physical universe. For example, a basic idea in physics is that the distance you travel over a specific amount of time is your velocity. If you're walking, you can travel one mile in about 20 minutes. So in one hour you'll travel three miles. That's "three miles an hour." In Ready, we measure velocity in "meters per second" or "m/s." So an object can be set to move across the screen at "1 m/s."

1. Place an object on screen.
2. Give it the bullet behavior.
3. Set the bullet behavior to be 1 m/s.
4. Leave the angle at its default direction, pointing straight to the right.

Your object should move to the right and off screen.

1. Zoom out to 50%.
2. Play again.

It seems your object is moving more slowly, but that's an illusion. By zooming out, you're able to see it travel farther. It now takes twice as long to get to the end of the screen, because it's traveled twice as far.

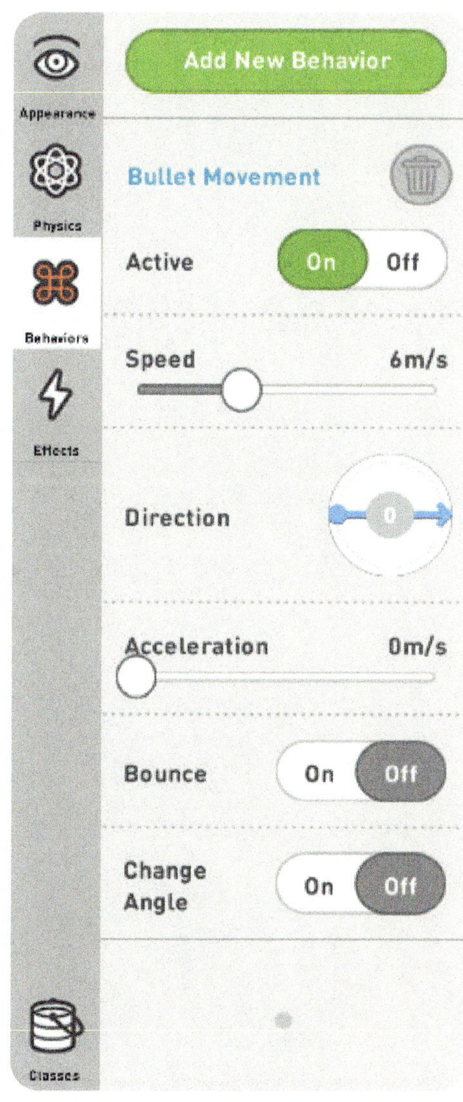

Let's understand velocity as a function of movement over distance.

1. Place an object on screen.
2. Activate physics, with gravity on.

The object should fall off screen. But in reality, it's continuing to fall past the viewport forever (or until you stop the program).

Let's get a sense of its speed. Now add some code.

1. "When the object's physics velocity is greater than 10, do system global set color red."

The object should fall off screen, and eventually the screen should become red (or whatever color you set). The object is continuing to accelerate. You could set a second command:

1. "When the object's velocity is greater than 20, do system global set color green."

You'll notice the time it took for the object to go from red to green was faster than from white to red. That's because the object is accelerating through space. Measuring how fast the object is speeding up is the basis of calculus. Calculus is math that describes how things change over time. In Ready, you experience these deep concepts naturally, by changing settings and feeling how, in turn, that changes the way the scene works.

EXPERIMENT!
MEASURING VELOCITY

1. Add an object to the scene.
2. In **Appearance**, set solid "off."
3. Turn **physics** on and set **gravity** on.
4. Make the object weigh 1,000 kilograms (about 2,200 pounds).
5. Copy the object with the little "+" button.
6. The second object should be exactly on top of the first one.
7. Open **physics** for the second object, with **gravity** on and a mass of 1 kg.
8. Zoom out to 50%.
9. Press play.

It should look like one object is falling. Are you surprised? Did you think the heavier object would fall faster than the lighter object? You'll notice we turned solid "off." If we'd left solid "on" then the two objects would "rub against" each other, and the friction between them would change their relative speed, and one would wind up falling ahead of the other. Friction is another way of saying "drag," or air resistance.

Let's create the effect of air resistance.

Carefully slide one object to the side of the other (it doesn't matter which one).
For the object you slid over, change **physics / drag** to 50%.

The object now falls much slower than the other! You've recreated the experience of traveling through a medium, like air, water, or molasses, depending on how far you set the drag.

MIND BENDER

If you drop a feather and a steel ball from the same height in a room with no air – a vacuum – they'll both hit the floor at the same time! If you try this at home, the ball will land first. Why? Because the air in the room is creating resistance, or "drag," that slows down the feather more than the ball. If you jump out of an airplane, the same thing happens to you. Near the surface of the Earth, an object in freefall in a vacuum will accelerate at approximately 9.8 m/s^2, independent of its mass. With air resistance acting on an object that has been dropped, the object will eventually reach a terminal velocity, which is around 53 m/s (195 km/h or 118 mph) for a human skydiver.

IV. HELLO WORLD!
LIFE IN READY

The real fun begins when objects on screen interact with each other, and with you. The interaction between things and people can be considered a form of life. As with living things, they can be simple or complex. The limit is set by you, their designer.

MOTORS

Let's begin by controlling a motor.

1. In the library, find a **gear**. Tip: You can search "gear."
2. Put the gear on screen.
3. Activate **physics** with gravity on.
4. Now get a flat, straight platform.
5. Put it under the gear so that the gear is almost on top of the platform.
Under **Appearance**, stretch the platform to be really long. Say 20 on the x-axis.
6. When you press play, the gear should rest on the platform.
Program: "When platform sensing touch held, do gear's physics add torque clockwise 5."

When you tap the platform, the gear should start rolling. The longer you hold down, the faster the gear will move. Release the platform and the gear slows down. Why? Because the weight of the gear on the platform creates friction, and the friction, over time, will slow the gear down if it's no longer being propelled by your "touch down" command. That's the same way cars work: Turn on the motor to push the car forward; turn off the motor and the car will slow down and come to a stop from the friction between the tires and the road (assuming it's a flat road; on a hill it will behave differently).

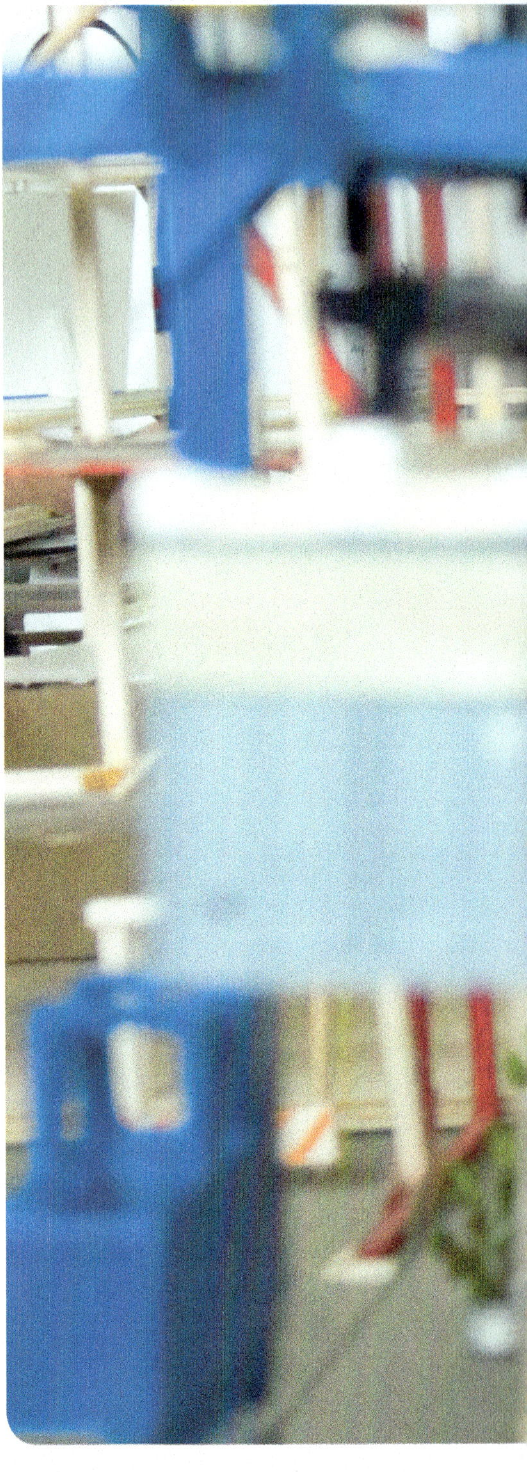

Go ahead and experiment with a few ideas to see how they affect the gear's speed:
- Change the **drag** on the gear.
- Change the gear's mass — make it heavier, and then lighter.
- Under **appearance**, change the gear's **material** from none to the various options you see.
- Now change the platform's material — make it **icy** for example.

All these things affect the friction between the gear and the platform.
- Reset back to something close to where this experiment began.
- The gear should roll to the right.
- Select the gear and in appearance, **swap visual**. Replace the gear image with a **bordered circle** from basic shapes.

The object now rolls without bouncing as much — that's because it has no edges like the gear. It's smooth. You could create the same effect by leaving the gear image alone, and under **appearance / collider** selecting **circle** instead of **polygon**. This creates an imaginary circle around the gear.

1. Continue exploring this scene. Add more platforms, and turn some of them to go upwards. Now the gear is climbing a hill.
2. Turn some to go downwards. If the gear is moving too fast, build in a brake: "When gear's velocity is greater than [some number], do add relative torque counterclockwise."

Now the gear should be self-correcting. It won't accelerate past a certain speed.
1. Add a lot of zigzagging platforms by copying them.
2. Say, **"When system scene starts, do camera follow smoothly gear."**

Now wherever the gear goes, the camera follows it. Go ahead and decorate your scene: Add a trail effect to the gear, change the background. Make it your own.

HINGES

Let's play with some built-in Ready motors, beginning with hinges.

1. Add a **bordered circle** to the scene.
2. Add a **bordered rectangle**.
3. Rotate the rectangle so it's long from side to side.
4. Put the rectangle to the right of the circle.
5. Add a **hinge behavior** to the circle.
6. Join it to the rectangle.

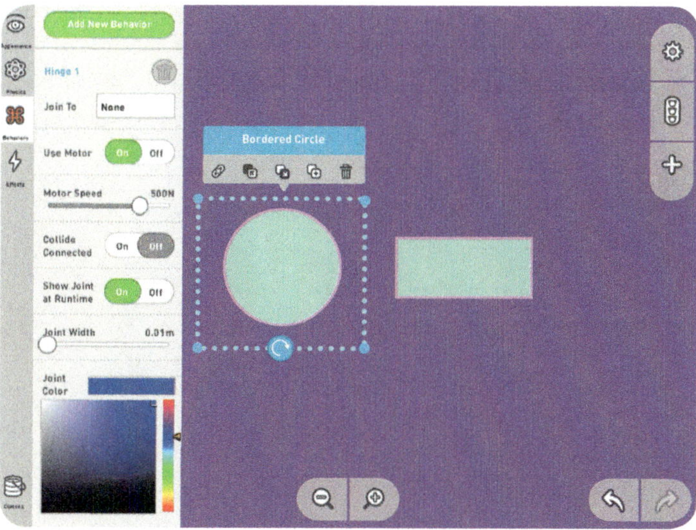

MIND BENDER

Newtons are named after Isaac Newton (1646 - 1726), an English mathematician who discovered gravity. Newton claims he came to understand the force of gravity by seeing an apple fall from a tree. In the apocryphal version, the apple fell on Newton's head. In Ready's Event Manager, we represent setting gravity on or off with a falling apple.

Now the rectangle rotates around the circle. Changing the motor speed will change the rectangle's speed, and eventually its direction, from clockwise to counterclockwise.

1. Add a **hinge behavior** to the rectangle.
2. Connect it to the circle.
3. Remove the hinge behavior from the circle.

Now the circle turns around the rectangle. What do you think will happen if you give them both hinge behaviors and connect each to the other? In Ready, you learn by doing, so give it a try.

Whichever object is spinning is the **child**. The object with the behavior is the **parent**. The Earth spins around the sun, so the sun is our parent. The moon spins around the Earth, so it's our child.

1. Activate **physics** and **change the mass** and drag on the child.

Now it should spin at a different velocity. The weight and drag counteracts the force, measured in **newtons**, of the motor. It takes more energy to move a heavy object. So newtons are the calculation of the **force** (energy) required to move an object of a certain **mass** (weight). A newton is the amount of force needed to move a 1 kilo object 1 meter.

EXPERIMENT!

MODEL OUR SOLAR SYSTEM

1. Add the sun in the center.
2. Place eight circles in a line from the sun.
3. Name each circle after a planet, with the first being Mercury.
4. **Add eight hinges to the sun.**
5. Attach each hinge to a planet.
6. With the same motor speed, the planets closer to the sun should make one orbit faster than the ones farther away.
7. Add a moon to the Earth, by giving Earth its own hinge connected to the moon.

You've made a solar system!

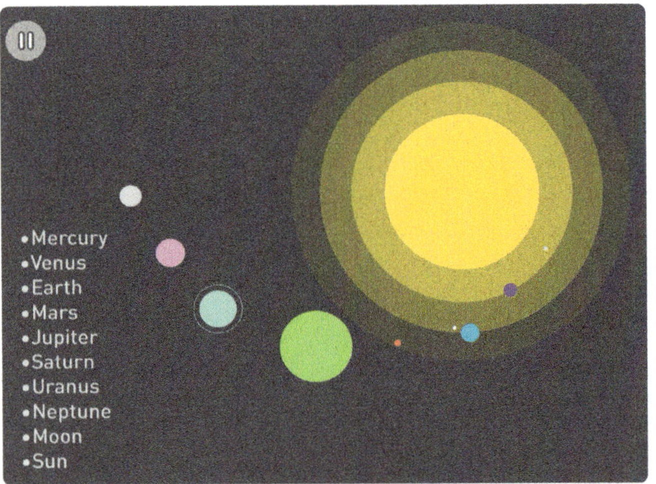

Look carefully at how the Earth behaves relative to its moon. There's a wobble. In your model, that wobble may be very obvious. It's the force of the moon pulling on the Earth. In real life, the moon's pull on the Earth wobbles the oceans, which slosh around producing high and low tides!

Bonus round:

1. Add a line running up and down through the sun.
2. Set the line solid / off.
3. Call the line Year Counter.
4. From **Interface & Text**, add a **score label** for each planet. Make sure that the score labels are solid / off as well. Name each one after a planet, e.g. **Mercury Year** for Mercury.
5. Line them up in a row on the left side of the screen with Mercury's first, and down from there.
Now each time a planet "senses collided with object Year Counter, do that planet's score label add 1."

Voila! You can see how many years pass on each planet, relative to the other. Mercury's year should go the fastest: 88 Earth days is one Mercury year.

The sun is 109 times larger than the Earth, and 330,000 times denser! This density is what produces nuclear fusion, compressing hydrogen atoms to a point where they convert their mass into energy. That energy is what we experience as sunlight. Mind Bender: The sun is an unshielded nuclear reactor. Every time you look at the sun, you're looking at a massive nuclear power plant emitting stupendous amounts of energy. That's one reason why it hurts to look at it.

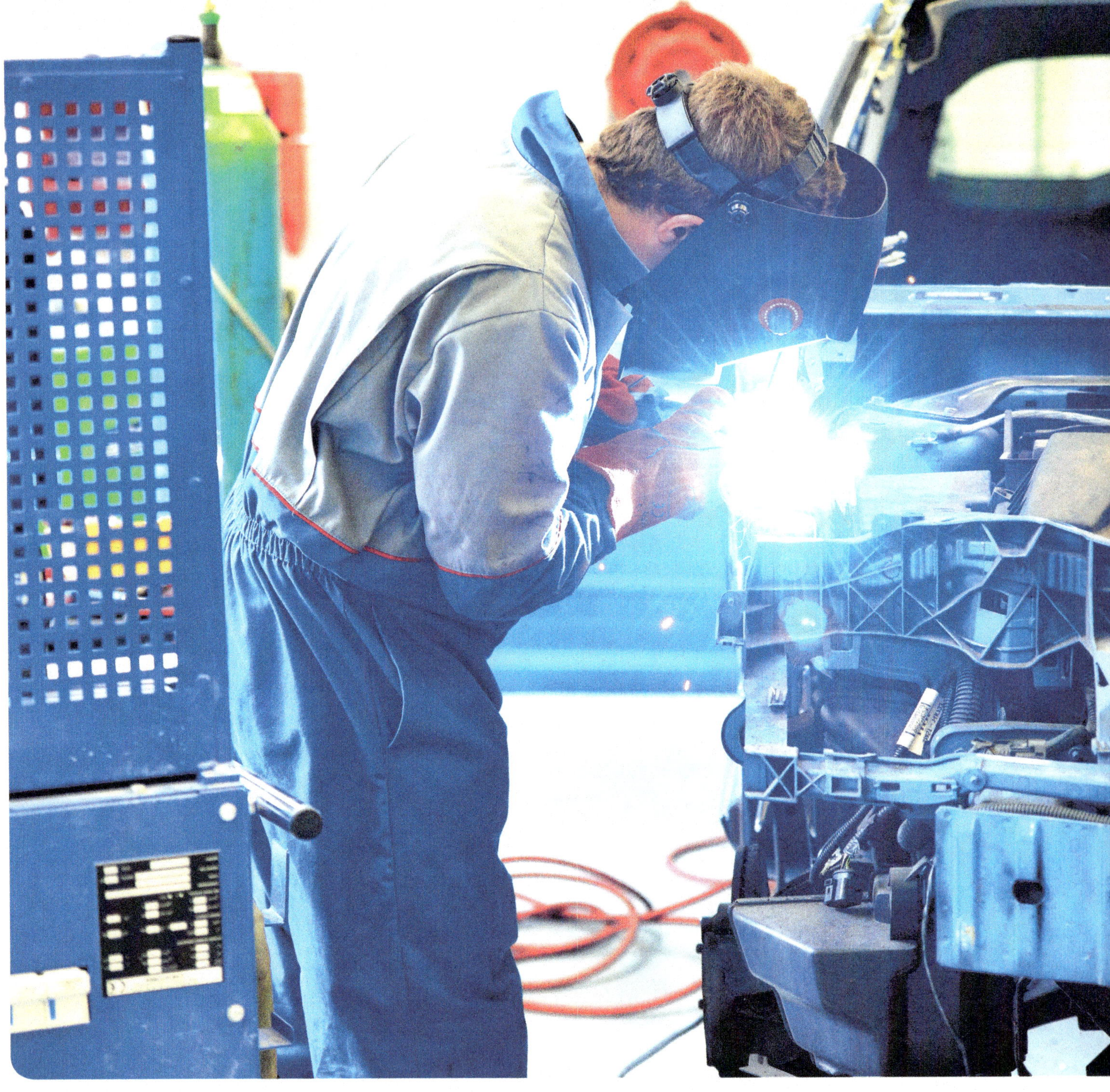

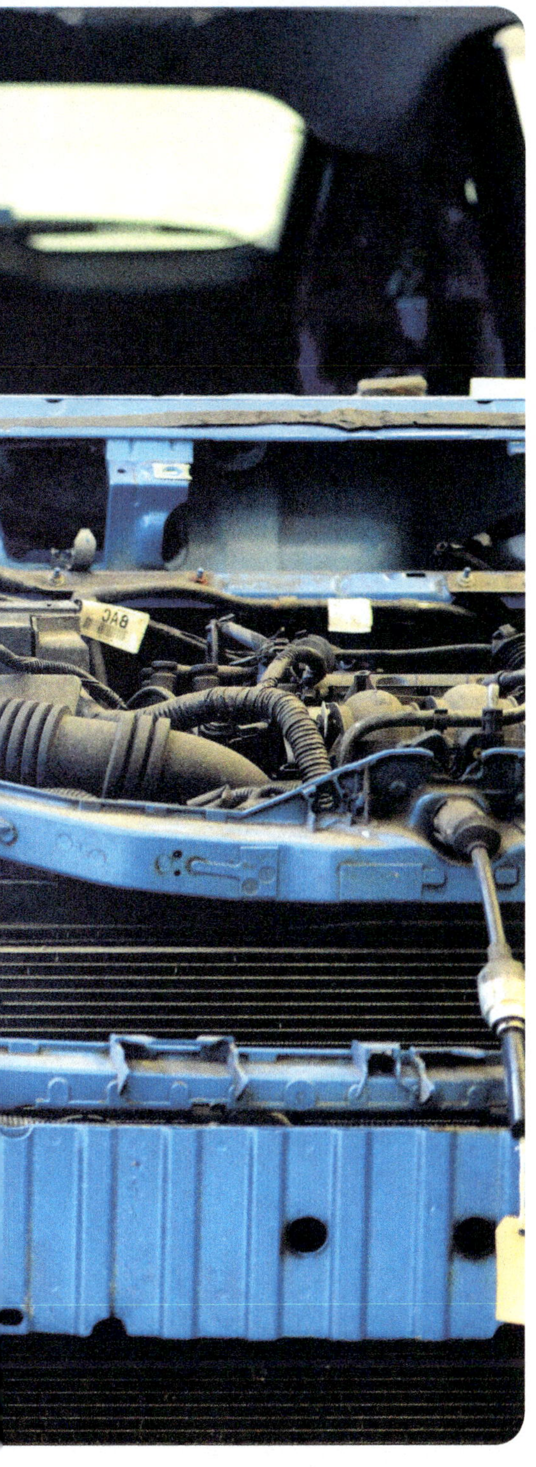

EXPERIMENT!

BUILD A CAR

A joint can become a wheel. Let's build a car.

1. Add a rectangular object to the scene. This is the body of your car.

2. Add a platform below it. This is the road. Stretch it out lengthwise.

3. Add two circular objects to the scene. These are wheels. Name them **wheel-L** and **wheel-R** for the left and right wheels.

4. Add a plain button from **Interface & Text** to the scene.

- Call it **accelerator** and set the text under **appearance** to read **FASTER**.
- Under **Appearance**, set the button in the layer **user interface**.

5. For the two circular objects, prep them to become wheels:

- Put them under the car.
- Give both wheels a **joint behavior**.
- Set the joint behavior to be at 90 degrees, angle / off.
- Turn the **show joint at runtime** off.

6. Command, "When accelerator button sensing touch held, do wheel-L, add relative torque clockwise 10N."

FASTER!

You now have a vehicle that acts like a car, with real-wheel drive. You may notice your car is very unstable, and flips over. Fix that by experimenting with the car's physics:

1. For the car, turn on **physics**.
2. Gravity on.
3. Lock **rotation**.

Now the car should stabilize and... drive!

Go ahead and customize your scene:
- Swap visual assets on the car body and wheels to make it your own.
- Set a background.
- Give the car a smoke or trail effect.
- Have the camera follow the car.
- Copy the road and make obstacles: ramps, cliffs. You now have a daredevil game!

EXPERIMENT!
RUBBERBAND

A very popular **game mechanic** is the slingshot. In Angry Birds, birds are launched towards pigs using a slingshot. A slingshot has these characteristics:

- **Launcher:** This is the frame that holds an imaginary rubber band.
- **Rubberband:** It can be pulled back, and depending on how far back, will propel a missile.
- **Missile:** This is what goes onto the rubberband.
- **Launch event:** firing the missile once it's pulled back.
- **Reloader:** a mechanism to put the next missile into the slingshot.

Let's go ahead and build a basic slingshot.

1. Add two objects to the screen. One is the missile. The other is the launcher.
2. The launcher is the **parent**, and gets a **rubberband behavior**. Connect the behavior to the missile (the child).
3. Give the missile a **drag behavior** so you can pull it.
Play the scene.

You can tune the rubberband between the missile and the launcher by changing the elasticity of the rubberband in meters. This defines how far the band can be extended. The farther it extends, the more force it sends into the missile when released. Activating physics on the missile allows you to tune how it behaves once released. Activating gravity tells the missile to fly in a parabolic arc; it will be pulled down over time. Drag will affect its velocity, as will mass.

Once released, the missile remains connected to the rubberband. Let's unjoin it, to launch.

Write, "When missile sensing touch up, do launcher's rubberband unjoin."

The touch up event is a very useful way to sense a person's intention. It's triggered when they stop touching an object. In this case, when someone stops holding the missile, it breaks the rubberband so that it can launch into space.

Now a new problem emerges— reloading the launcher. Depending on the scene, you'll need to decide what triggers loading the next missile. Let's assume that when the missile is out of sight, it's time load the next one:

When missile sensing seen no, do missile's position set to launcher, **and** launcher's rubberband join to missile.

Now whenever the missile disappears, it's brought back and **reconnected to the launcher**.

Congratulations! You have a slingshot.

4 - Left
0 - Hits

EXPERIMENT!
LAUNCHING ONTO A PLATFORM

Slingshots are good at two things: hitting an object either to destroy it (as in Angry Birds) or to intercept it. An example of the latter is the circus act where a clown is placed in a canon (a kind of slingshot) and launched in the air — the trick is to land precisely on a target.

Continue with your scene:

1. Add an object, like a platform, below the slingshot. Adjust your scene as necessary. You may need to zoom out to give enough space.

Now try to launch your missile and have it land on top of the platform. If it's too hard, tune the missile's physics. Some ideas:

1. Change the missile's **mass** and **drag**, for instance, so it flies in a more predictable arc.
2. Change the **elasticity** of the rubberband — the smaller, the less power.
3. Turn off **collide connected** in the rubberband behavior, so the missile won't crash against the launcher. Or leave it on, if it's part of the game.

FRANKE

For now, let's assume it's hard to land on the platform, so just accomplishing it once is a **win moment**. Let's count how many tries it takes to land successfully, and then launch fireworks when you do.

1. Add a **score label** from **Interface & Text**.
2. Add a **fireworks effect** to the platform; set active no.
3. Add a new command to the existing event that reloads the launcher: "And do score label's score add 1."

Each time you launch and fail to land, a new missile is reloaded and the scene counts what try you're on to.

Celebrate landing on the platform and stop the game:

1. When the missile sensing touching platform do:
- Missile's physics reset velocity (this stops the missile from falling, rolling, or bouncing off the platform).
- Platform's fireworks effect set active yes.
You might like the challenge of landing perfectly on the platform. In that case, don't reset the missile's velocity. You might need to further tune drag and mass to make this a realistic accomplishment.

Once the basic mechanic is in place, optimizing the scene can begin. Some things to consider exploring:

- The platform can move. Give it a **bullet** behavior, and have it bounce between two walls on each end of the screen. These can be in the scene, or moved out of the scene, to add a bit more mystery as to when the platform returns. Set bullet behavior **bounce** to on. This will reverse the platform when it collides against a wall.
- The platform can rotate: Attach it to a new object with the **hinge** behavior, so it behaves like a Ferris wheel. The trick is to land as it travels in a circle.
- Change the position of the platform, above or below the launcher.
- Give the missile a **stay in frame** behavior. Does this change the game experience for better or worse?

SPAWNING SURVIVAL

In Angry Birds, the objective is not to land on a platform, but to strike a pig. This requires creating a stream of target objects. Spawning is a concept that describes the creation of objects, such as "bad piggies" or "enemy spaceships."

Spawning has these basic characteristics:
- A **spawn point** that manufactures the object.
- A object that is often **cloned** from a **master object**.
- A **class** to describe and detect the cloned object.
- A **spawn condition**: the logic that generates a new object. Often this is linked to a **random number generator** or a timer that plays a role in creating new objects in ways the player can't predict.

Remix or tune your existing launcher project to spawn target objects.

1. Place an object on screen. Call it **spawn point**.
2. Place another object on screen. Call it **target**.
3. Give the target a bullet behavior, and have it travel horizontally (left or right).
4. Place the target in a new class called **target**.
5. "When system runtime repeat every second, do spawn point clone target."
6. "When any object in target class sensing seen no, do target class remove affected clone."

Every second you should see a target object emerge from the spawn point and travel across the screen. You might notice the target object getting stuck on the spawn point. Since they're both defaulted to solid objects, they rub against each other. For the spawn point, set appearance solid off. Now it should produce a steady stream of clones.

Memory management requires that unnecessary clones be removed from the scene. In this case, once the clone has moved off screen, it can be destroyed. This won't work if the spawn point is off screen.

1. Move the spawn point off screen.

Now nothing seems to happen. The target objects, cloned off screen, are sensed as not seen on creation, and are immediately destroyed. Change the clone removal to be time based.

1. "When target class runtime existed longer than 3 seconds, do affected object from target class, clone remove clone."

Now after three seconds, the clone is removed.

1. Tune your scene so that a stream of target objects is within reach of the launcher.

2. Add a score label. Call it hits. Consider turning appearance solid off, as otherwise missiles will collide against the score label. Or leave it solid, if you like the effect.

"When missile sensing collided with any in class target, do score label's score add 1."

You're successfully launching towards a stream of targets. Let's tune this scene to create a consequence for missing a target.

1. Add a new score label. Call it missiles.

2. Set the score label's value to 3.

3. Find the launch command and a new event on launch:

- And missile score label's label, subtract 1.

4. Find your launcher reload command and add a new test for the When statement:

- And missile score label's value is greater than 0.

After 3 launches, you won't reload. The game's challenge is to hit as many targets as possible with only 3 missiles, as tracked by the hits score label.

Tune your scene by considering:

- Spawning different types of targets, with different speeds. Harder-to-hit targets generate more hit points in your score.
- Spawn power-up targets that if added to your missile total, will let you keep playing past 3 launches. If 3 launches to start is too hard, start with more. But be careful! A game that's too easy is boring.
- Create more than one spawn point so targets come from different areas of the screen.
- If the game feels too predictable, experiment by adding a **random number generator** behavior to an object. Based on the random number generated, chose one of several spawn points to generate a target. For example, random number 1 spawns at Spawn1, random 2 Spawn2, and so forth. **Name objects and events well**, to track these combinations.

RANDOM NUMBERS 

In one way or another, nearly all computer games use random numbers to help create a sense of **unpredictability**. The alternative, predictability, might sound compelling, but, it turns out, makes for boring games. Take for example a **match-3 game**, like Candy Crush, where the objective is to match three or more candies in a row. If it were obvious what the next candy is, most people wouldn't bother playing.

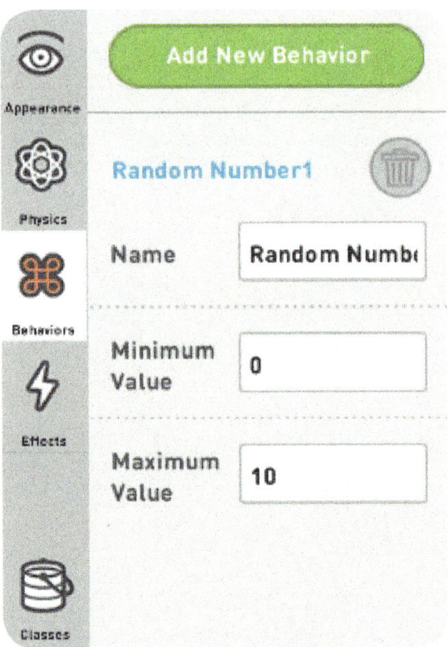

FUN FACT

The human brain is designed to pay special attention to new, unexpected events. Evolutionary biologists speculate that part of our success as a species is tied to our exceptional capability to detect patterns, and exploit them.

Picture early homo erectus, a million years ago, who couldn't run faster than most predators, and had no claws or sharp teeth. Yet, this unimpressive little animal managed to haul itself onto the top of the food chain. Pattern recognition was central to the success of our species.

Pattern recognition is what tells us that when there are bird droppings under a tree, perhaps a bird's nest, with tasty eggs, may lie above in the branches — worth a climb to see! Pattern recognition is a virtuous cycle; when focused on the right problems, like finding food, it leads to more energy for the brain, and more pattern recognition. Language itself is a high-level form of pattern recognition — what are words but patterns of sounds, which are recognized as having meaning between people who speak the same language? If pattern recognition is something people are exceptionally good at, in part that's because we are hard-wired to be rewarded for detecting patterns.

Brain scientists who map mental activity detect that when the brain sees a new or unexpected pattern, it pays special attention. It feels good to see a new pattern. If you didn't pay attention, you might miss the next big thing — say agriculture from those seeds you left on the ground that have sprouted plants bearing the same seeds that you dropped a year ago — or it could be a false alarm. Once a pattern is familiar, the dopamine release wanes, and eventually disappears altogether. The pattern's banked. The game is to move on and recognize the next pattern.

Random events, when they happen, create a surge of excitement in our minds: We are biologically trained to pay special attention to them. That's the secret to why so many games use random number generators. Without a sense of randomness, people get bored and abandon the game.

Abusing this mechanic is called a "hook loop." Gambling companies manufacture slot machines to keep players addicted to putting more money in. These gamified slots trick people into thinking they "almost won" when in fact they didn't come close. Ethical game designers are mindful of how the brain works, and design games to avoid exploiting our desire for unexpected patterns in ways that manipulate us into spending money. An analogy is sugar.

Some food companies put sugar into food, like hamburgers, to make them more addictive. Sugar also triggers a deep-seated chemical in the human brain, which tells us to want more when we taste sugar. We call this "junk food." Ethical food companies avoid manufacturing food that tricks our bodies into eating more than we should. The same can be said for apps. There are "junk apps" that exploit how our minds work to make us spend time and money on them.

By exposing these mechanisms for you to learn and control, Ready acts as a "whole food" for the brain, allowing us to understand what makes for healthy, and unhealthy, digital media.

8

EXPERIMENT!

MAGIC 8-BALL

Let's practice using a random number generator by making a version of the Magic 8-ball.

The Magic 8-ball was a toy. Inside the ball is a twenty-sided dice floating in blue jelly. You'd ask the ball a question like, "Will there be a snow day tomorrow?" Shake the Magic 8-ball, and up would float 1 of 20 seemingly random answers — or were they?! The fun came from the absurdity of the question and the strange patterns that would (seem) to emerge in the actually random answers.

Let's build a simple version with just three answers: Yes, No, and Maybe.

1. Add a text object to the screen from **Interface and Text**. Call it **question**.

2. Edit the text object under **appearance / text** to read: "Ask me a question and tap for the answer."

3. Add a **random number behavior** to the text object.

4. Configure the random number to have a range of 1 - 3. This will generate numbers 1,2,3.

5. Add another text object to the scene called answer. Edit the text to be empty.

6. "When question sensing touch up, do generate random number."

DON'T
COUNT
ON IT
© Mattel

7. "When question's random number is equal to 1, do answer's text label set text 'Yes.'"
8. "When question's random number is equal to 2, do answer's text label set text 'No.'"
9. "When question's random number is equal to 3, do answer's text label set text 'Maybe.'"

Each click on the "Ask me a question and tap for the answer" text should generate one of three answers in the answer box. These should be unexpected. Once your scene is working, you can embellish it:

- Instead of three possible answers, increase them. A good place to get answers is Wikipedia under the Magic 8-ball entry. You'll need to adjust the random number generator to go from 1 to "n" where "n" is the number of possible answers. The original 8-ball called for 1 to 20.
- Think about cleaning up the user experience of how the questions are asked.
- Use a counter behavior to track the stage of the question: 1. Waiting to be asked; 2. Providing an answer. With the counter, you can change other aspects of the scene, by adding decorative objects that change depending on what stage of the question / answer process you're in.
- Create reactions for the different types of answers by adding characters and objects to the scene that appear / disappear depending on which random answer is generated.
- Instead of tapping the text to generate an answer, consider adding an object and launching / spinning it, then resetting for the next question. You can generate interesting effects using the transition behavior.

EXPERIMENT!
BALLISTIC MISSILE

Ready doesn't provide a built-in way to create the equivalent of a ballistic launcher, which uses explosive force to launch an object (as opposed to a slingshot which uses elasticity). By combining existing Ready behaviors, you can generate a device that shoots objects.

All ballistic launchers have the following components:

Launching object: typically a tube.
Explosive force: such as gunpowder.
Ballistic object: often made of metal, like a cannon ball.
Trigger event to generate the explosion and launch the projectile.
Reload process to arm the next object.

In Ready, we can model these components:
- Place a launching object on the screen, such as a spaceship.
- Add a ballistic object, such as a plain circle to the scene. Call it missile.
- Give the plain object a bullet behavior; angle it to go upward.
- Turn the missile's appearance solid off.
- Put the bullet in a class called missile.
- "When launching object sensing touch down, do launching object clone missile."

You should now have a basic ballistic launcher: Every time you tap the ship, it sends off a missile.

Optimize the performance of the missiles by destroying clones when no longer needed, either when they're off screen or after a certain number of seconds.

- Change the launching event to be another object that works like a button. That object can be placed under appearance into the user interface layer. Now if the scene moves around, the button will float above it. Note: User interface buttons don't zoom in or out with the canvas. They stay the same size, so you have to resize them manually.
- Give the launcher a **control behavior**, such as **Control Pad**. Configure the controls as necessary, such as side to side for for a ship shooting enemies coming down from the top.
- By merging the spawn ingredients for generating targets and random number generation, create unexpected waves of enemies.
- Add a **life meter** to the ship. Configure the life meter under **Appearance**. Program an event such that whenever the ship collides with a target, do life meter substract 1.
- Create a **lose moment** when the life meter gets to 0: Stop the ship from firing more missiles, de-activate the controls, and fly in some text from outside the scene saying **"GAME OVER."**

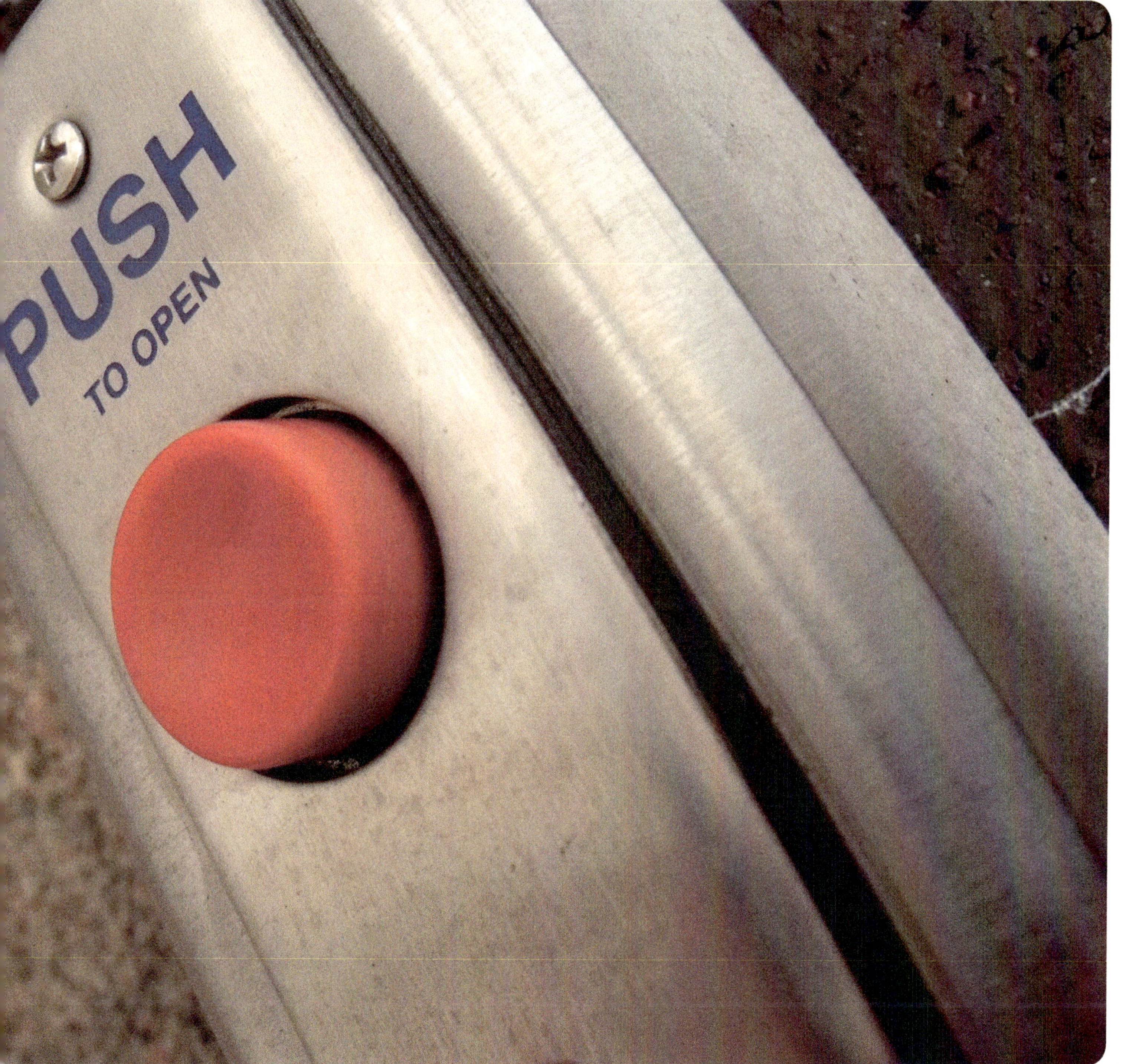
PUSH
TO OPEN

EXPERIMENT!

ROTATING CANNON

Let's build a more versatile launcher. This one rotates in a circle and shoots in every direction.

1. Add a circle to the screen. This acts as your rotating platform, to turn in a circle. Call it player.
2. Add a rectangle above it. Call it cannon.
3. Give the player the join-to behavior, and connect it to the cannon.
4. Create an event that says, "When player sensing touch held, do angle rotate clockwise 5 degrees."

Now the cannon should rotate clockwise when you press down on the circle, making the cannon launch a projectile.

1. Add an object to the scene to serve as a missile. Put it off to the side.
2. Put the missile object in a class called missile.
3. Turn physics on the missile, with gravity off.
4. "When shoot player sensing touch up, do cannon clone missile class, AND bullet class add relative force up 100N."

Now the player rotates as you hold it down, and when you let go, the player launches a missile.

- You can add three buttons to the scene for left turn, right turn, and shoot. Put them in the user interface layer, and rotate the player accordingly.
- You can take your cannon and place it on top of... a car. You now have a tank. Controlling this apparatus may be tricky!

Congratulations! You're approaching the level of a professional game designer!

V. USER INTERFACE

Any piece of software you use has a user interface. This describes the mechanism a person uses to interact with the software. In a writing app, the user interface includes the "ribbon" that shows "B" for bold and "I" for italics, the world "File" that generates a drop-down menu with file related options, such as "new" or "save."

Games have their own user interface styles. Much of the fun in a game is related to the design of the user interface. A basic game, such as Pong where you play tennis against the computer, is a great exercise in user interface design. Let's think about how Pong works.

- Start screen: where you might be asked whether you want "1 player" or "2 player." The 1 player version is you against the computer. The 2 player version is you against a friend.
- Game screen: the area where you play pong. It has two score counters: one for each player (human or computer).
- Level indicator / controller: if you win a game, you might progress to the next level, which is harder.
- Player controller: How you control your paddle. You might be dragging it with your hand, or using a joystick to move it.
- Game over screen: Once the game is finished, either because someone won or lost, an announcement is made. Typically the option is given to "play again."

Game designers spend a remarkable amount of time on user interfaces. It's often more difficult and time consuming than the design of the actual game. The same is true in Ready. That's because Ready is built on a professional-grade game engine called Unity. Game engines are amazing products: They provide game designers with physics engines to simulate the real world. Ready exposes a "2D physics engine." In the future, Ready might expose a 3D physics engine, to create a first-person experience where you can traverse a world, as in Minecraft.

Game engines typically favor quick results around physical mechanics. For example in Ready, saying physics on, gravity on, material bouncy, add behavior stay in frame with reaction reflect takes a few taps for an experienced maker. Then on play, a remarkably complex series of equations are solved, which makes the object bounce around the screen, nearly

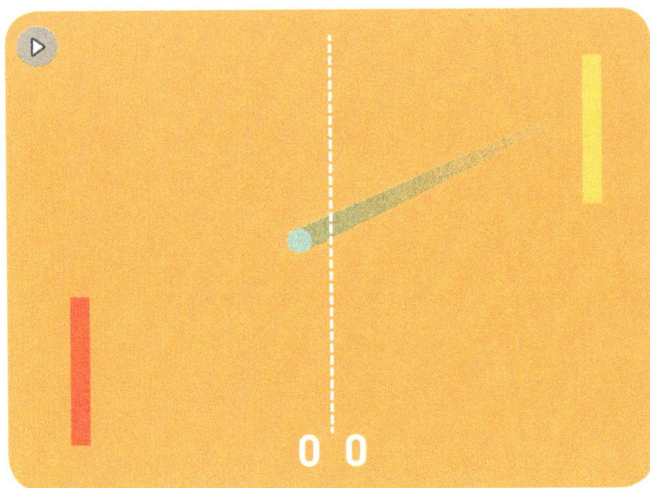

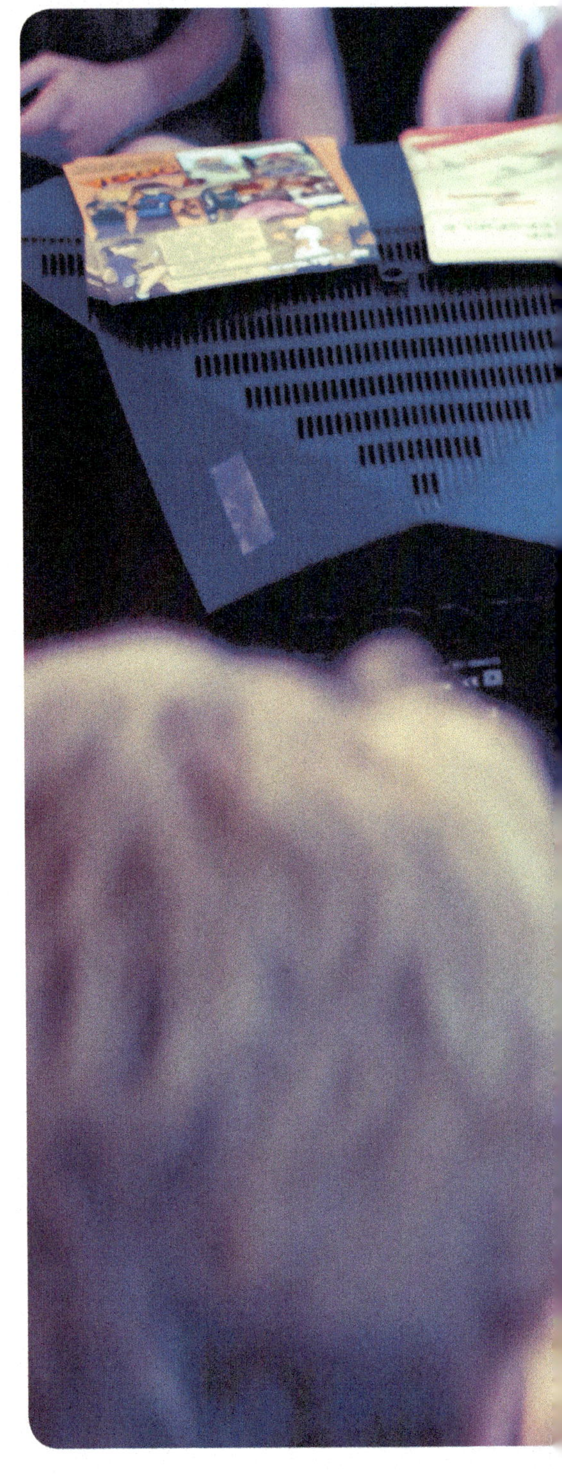

never in exactly the same way! Having to write the equations from scratch to generate this realistically, and then provide all the options to tune the mechanic, could easily take... a year! It took Unity many years of development, with many programmers working to arrive at their current physics engines. Thanks to their effort, the game engine handles modeling the world for you, leaving you free to do the creative work around the game mechanic, tuning the game play, and designing game art to put in the game.

User interface doesn't come out of the box in quite the same way as physics. Successful user interface design is a creative art, and requires, as with architecting a building, a lot of patience. It's best done step by step, rather than all at once. Testing the user interface is also essential (along with the overall game play), to make sure people understand at every moment where they are, and what they can do next.

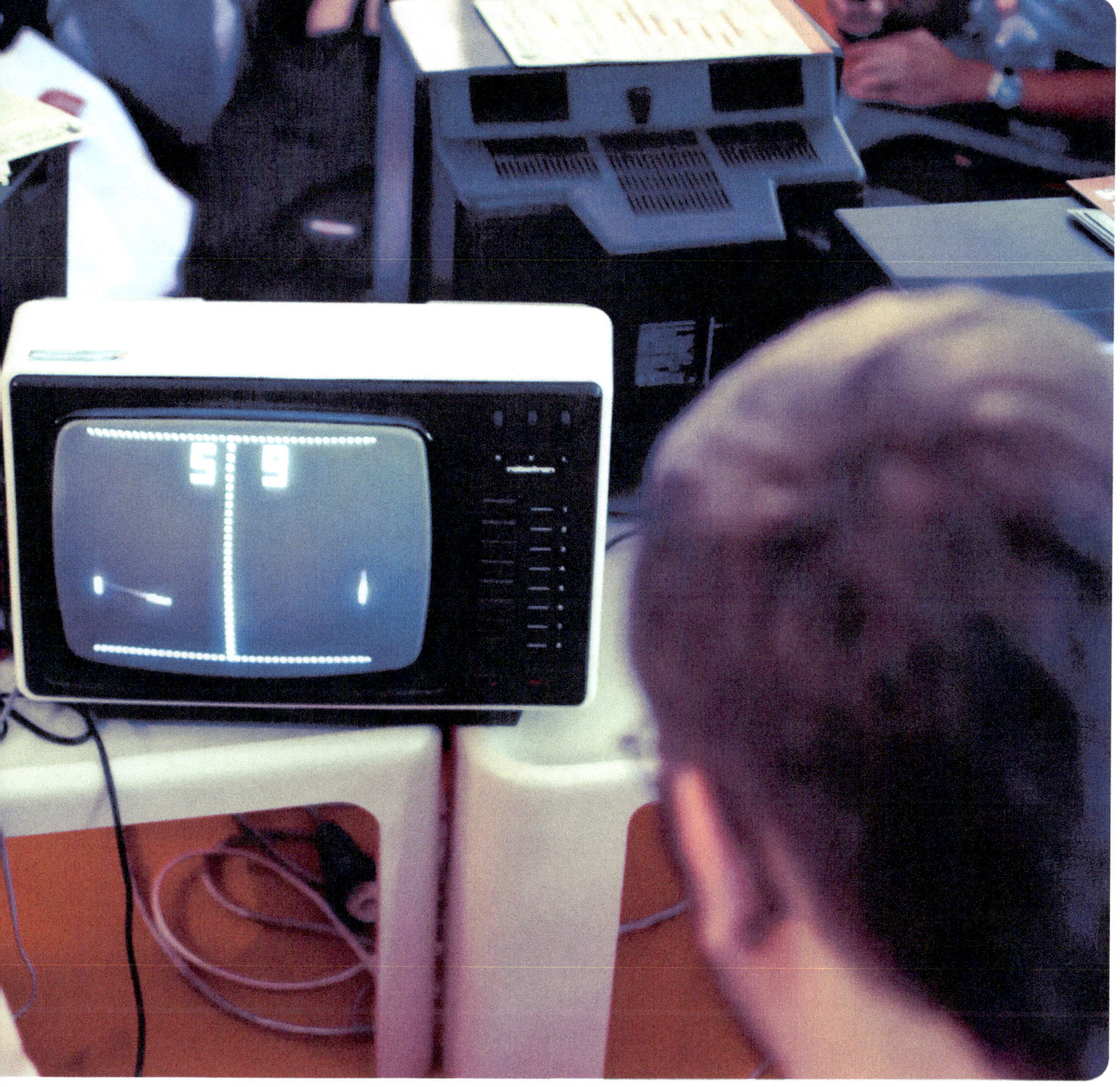

CENTRUM

LEVELS

In Ready, building a multi-screen user interface requires a new concept: levels.

Levels are stages in a game, but they're also stages in using the game.
- **Start level:** the start game screen, where you might configure your player, decide how many people are playing, and level of difficulty.
- **Level 1:** the first level of the game. This can lead to level 2 and all the way up to "n," where n is the highest potential level you can reach. For instance, the original arcade version of Donkey Kong had only 4 game levels.
- **Restart / end level:** the point where the player has ended the game, and can start over.

In Ready, you have an infinite canvas. Take a piece of paper, and imagine this is a zoomed out view of your canvas.

1. On the bottom left, draw a box the size of the screen if you were zoomed back in. Label this box Start Level.
2. Go up and to the right. Draw another box. This is level 1 of your game. Keep going up and to the right drawing boxes, labeling each level 1, level 2, and so on, up to the last level.
3. Put a final box and call it Game Over level.

4

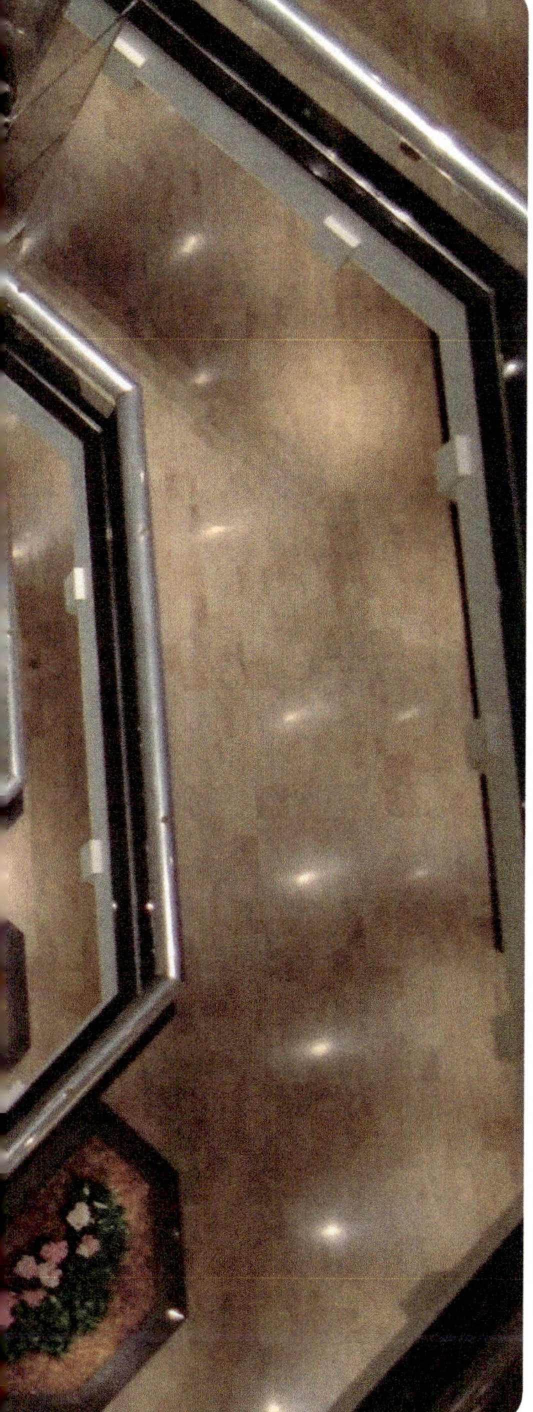

You should see a diagonal line going from the bottom left to the top right of your paper. This is the overall architecture of your game. Here's how you control the journey from box to box:

- Each level should have an anchor point. This is a visible or hidden object (appearance / set opacity to 0 will hide it) that can be used to tell the camera to go there on some condition. For example, "When start button sensing touch up, do camera position set position to Level-1-anchor-point."
- The overall game will likely need a state counter to track the "state of the game." States could include:

The player is on the start level, game not yet started.
The player is playing level 2; game active.
The player has lost, and is in the "Game Over" level.
The player is at "Game Over" and wants to restart the game.

When architecting the user interface, it's a good idea to start by sketching ideas on paper. This is sometimes called a wireframe or a project map. In some cases, designers design on blank wireframes that contain life-size cutouts of screens, like a phone screen, with dots indicating a certain amount of pixels between each one. This saves a lot of time, as a well-designed wireframe means less time is spent fiddling in the actual programming with the distance between objects. Ready is keyed to the aspect ratio of an Apple iPad, which is 1024 pixels across and 768 pixels tall. Searching for "blank iPad wireframe" will turn up a printable version that you can use to design individual Ready screens.

EXPERIMENT!
A MULTI-LEVEL GAME

Objects in Ready can be placed on one of three layers:

Scene: objects you can interact with.
Background: objects behind the scene objects. They can be affected, but can't collide with objects in the scene.
User interface: a layer in front of the scene, like a glass wall, where buttons can go. These also cannot collide with objects in the scene. They also don't move when the camera moves from one scene to another.

In this exploration, user interface can be used to tell a simple story. Let's build a project that has:

- **A start screen.**
- **Three levels.**
- **A game over screen.**

You'll want to organize your project by doing the following things to prepare:

1. Place an object in the center of the screen. Call it **level 0 anchor**.
2. Place a plain button on the screen and put it in the user interface layer in appearance.
3. Set the text in appearance to read **Start**.
4. Give the button a counter **behavior**. Name it **level**.
5. Copy the **level 0 anchor** and drag that copy up and to the right. Zoom out so you can easily move it there.
6. Name it **level 1 anchor**. Repeat this process three more times for **level 2**, **level 3**, and **game over**.
7. In the **Event Manager** write an **event**: "When start button sensing touch up, do start button's level add 1."
8. Write a series of events: "When start button's level counter = 1, camera set position to level 1 anchor." Repeat this for level 2, 3, and end game (level 4). You can use the "+" button in the Event Manager to copy the event and then modify the parameters.
9. At level 4, if the user clicks the button, go back to level 0 and reset the button's counter to 0.

Playing your scene, the camera should jump from

one level to the next each time it's tapped, and then wrap back to the start.
You might think that Level 0 and Level 4 feel redundant. Isn't level 4 just ... a version of level 0? That depends.

At the "Game Over" level you can give the option to **try again**. If "yes," then send the person to Level 1. If "no," then go to Level 0!

In a game where a score was accumulated across Levels 1, 2, and 3 , Level 4 would play a distinct role as a **win / lose** moment, potentially tabulating achievements. From there, the player returns to the Start level (level 0), reset all achievements, and have the option of playing again, and possibly configuring game parameters, like the overall difficulty (easy, medium, hard).

This is why mapping out the overall architecture on paper is so important. It helps you understand whether you need "intro" and "outro" screens, or even intermediate screens between levels!

STATE COUNTERS

Even more complex is the interaction between levels. One reason for placing the levels in a staircase format is that any object moving side-to-side or up-and-down won't crash into another level! Strange to think of, but it's possible that an object in one scene could fall into another scene, and create unintended consequences.

For this reason, many games have internal logic that turns objects on and off, based on whether the player is in the level or not. For example, if each level spawns enemies, it would bog down the computer to tell it to spawn enemies that the camera isn't even looking at! Not only could these enemies potentially make sounds or movements that interfere with the current level, they also would slow down the overall game play, as the computer would be doing all these other calculations off screen.

An easy way to turn everything on or off is to use the anchor point as the level start trigger.

When anchor point sensing seen "yes," do [activate a bunch of level events like spawning enemies]. Implied in this command is what not to do when not seen: Don't spawn any enemies.

In more complex situations the "seen" command may need to be augmented with a special **state counter** that, based on a number, also controls whether things are turned on and off. In the project we just tried, the button's state counter can potentially serve to do this. This is a **global state counter**. However, it may be that each level should have a **local state counter** that does additional work turning things on and off. Mapping all this out on paper is essential, as it can get quite complex to wing it!

← TO TACOMA.
PHONE.
MARKER
PHONE
MARKER
PHONE.
MARKER.
TO SEATTLE
FROM TO REVERSE FROM TO REVERSE
A B 2A 2B G H 26
C D 1A
E F 7 3 G M 17 24 14
E G 6 7 3 I H 13 23
I M 17 13 23 14
M L 15
C.M.ST.P.&P.R.R.
P.C.R.
AMPERES D.C.
WESTON
VOLTS
BROTHERHOOD OF RAILROAD SIGNALMEN

FEEDBACK

All user interfaces orient you to where you are in the journey, and whether your command has been received. Ways to do this include:

- Changing the color of a button where you are tapping it.
- Making a sound when you click something.
- Changing the size of something when you're selecting or de-selecting it.

In your multi-level scene, add some feedback:

- When the button is tapped, change the color under appearance for the down state.
- Make a sound when the button's tapped.
- Add a text object next to each level anchor. Name the text objects clearly, like "Level 1 text."
- To the events that move the camera to an anchor point, append another action: "Level 1 text, append text 'Welcome to level 1.'" Modify the welcome text for each level.

VI. PUTTING IT ALL TOGETHER

Ready
Maze

Ready Maze
Level: Beginner

We're going to build a maze in Ready. In this project, we'll create a **CHARACTER** who starts at **HOME BASE** that needs to follow a **PATH** and avoid **OBSTACLES** to get a **PRIZE**. To win, the character must bring the prize back to home base. In this maze, the character isn't allowed to touch the **OBSTACLES**. If they do, they will be "zapped" and have to start over from **HOME BASE**.

STEPS TO BUILD

1. Add PLAYER
2. Add PRIZE
3. Add HOME BASE
4. Set BACKGROUND
5. Add an OBSTACLE
6. Create the "Obstacle class" and Copy
7. Give PLAYER behavior and effects
8. Set HOME BASE & PRIZE
9. Set up the OBSTACLES, PLAYER & PRIZE
10. Add TIMER
11. Event #1: Pick up the PRIZE
12. Event #2: Zap PLAYER when touching OBSTACLE
13. Event #3: Win and stop TIMER when PRIZE is back home.
14. BONUS: Make your game harder by switching "ON" "Physics"
15. BONUS: Give your game a time limit

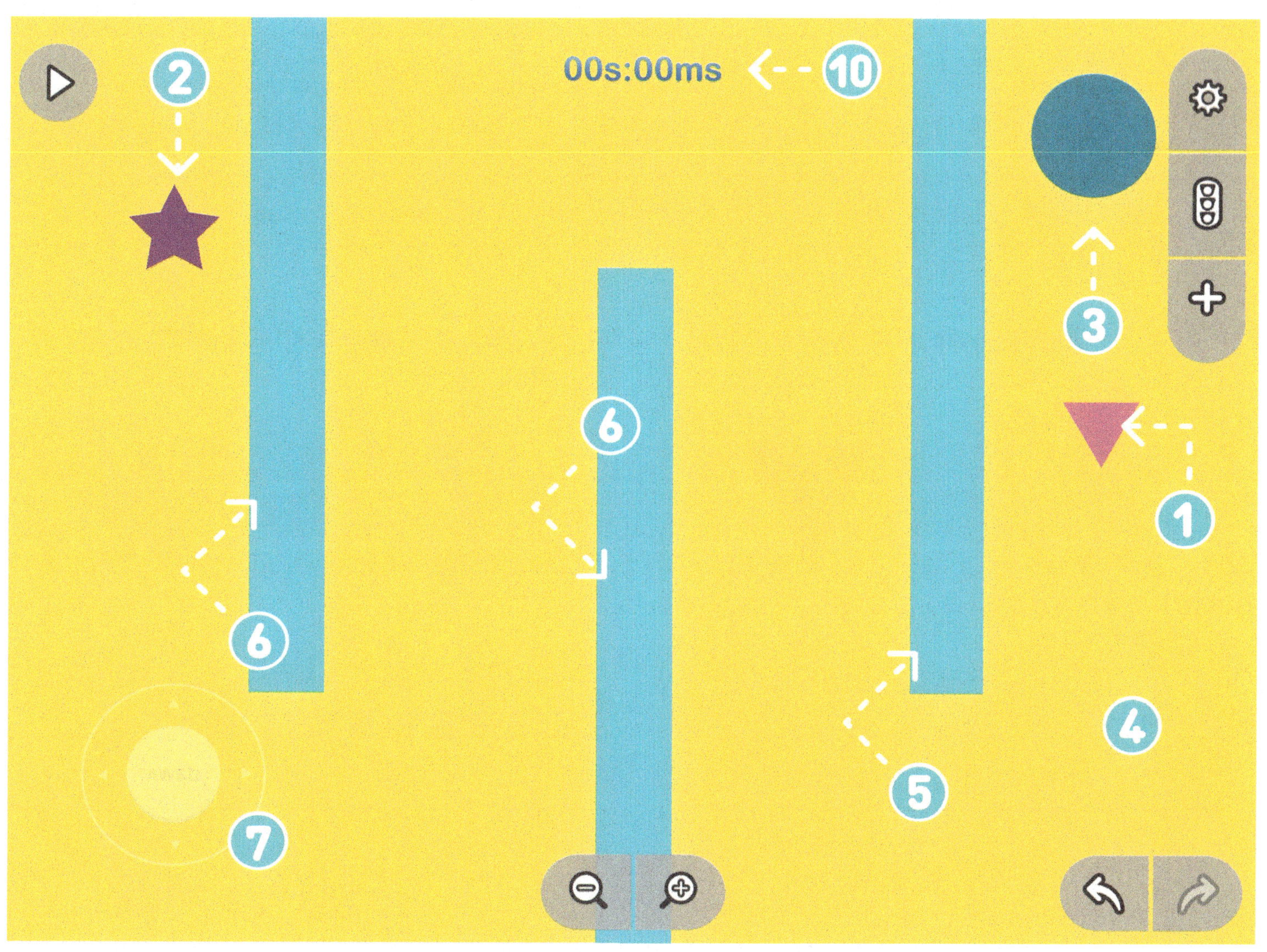
2
00s:00ms
10
3
6
1
6
4
5
7

ADD PLAYER

The Player is the main character in our maze game.

1. Go to the **Artwork** tab in the **Library.**

2. Name it in the **Appearance** tab in the **Inspector**.

2

ADD PRIZE

By making the prize "not-solid" the Player will be able to pick it up.

1. Go to the **Artwork** tab in the **Library**

2. Name it and make it **not solid** in the **Appearance** tab in the **Inspector**

ADD HOME BASE

By making it "not-solid" and translucent we will be able to see through it and spawn our Player when it gets "zapped".

1. Go to the **Artwork** tab in the **Library**.

2. Name it + Make it not solid from the **Appearance** tab in the **Inspector**.

3. Make it 50% transparent from the **Appearance** tab in the **Inspector**.

SET BACKGROUND

Don't worry if it's not perfect. It can be changed again later.

1. Drag any background and drop it on your canvas from the **Background** tab in the **Library**.

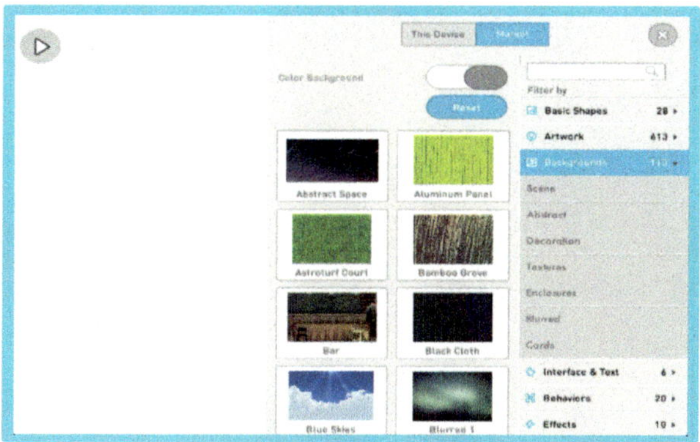

ADD OBSTACLE

Use this as the wall in our maze. By hiding it from the event manager it won't clutter up the project.

1. Go to the the **Basic Shapes** tab in the **Library**.

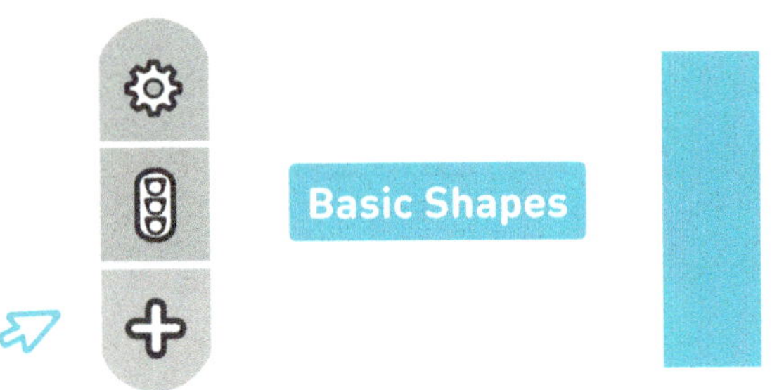

2. Hide it from your event manager: from the **Appearance** tab in the **Inspector**.

CREATE OBSTACLE CLASS AND COPY

Classes are a way that we can give instructions to objects as a group instead of as individuals. Since we want to have many obstacles it makes sense to do it.

1. Select the **OBSTACLE**, then tap **Create New Class** in the **Bucket icon** at the bottom of the **Inspector**.

2. Copy the **OBSTACLE 3** times and lay them out in maze fashion.

GIVE PLAYER BEHAVIORS

Give the player the ability to move around the screen with a controller and prevent it from leaving the frame of the scene. Add the Impact effect to trigger it each time the player touches an obstacle.

1. **Control pad** (with change angle) from the **Behavior** tab in the **Inspector**.

2. **Stay in frame** Behaviors (on collide) from the **Behavior** tab in the **Inspector**.

3. **Impact Effect** (on Zap): from the **Behavior** and **Effects** tabs in the **Inspector**.

EXPERIMENT

Now that the user can control the character, test your setup so far. Press the play button

TRY THIS

1. Move the character to the obstacles. What happens?
2. Move the character to the Home Base. What happens?

SET HOME BASE & PRIZE

Don't worry that it looks too easy. Spice things up later to make it harder.

1. Set your **HOME BASE** and **PRIZE** in opposite ends of your scene.

SET UP OBSTACLES, PLAYER & PRIZE

Don't worry that it looks to easy. Spice things up later to make it harder

1.Set up your **OBSTACLES** and adjust your **PLAYER** & **PRIZE** accordingly.

ADD A TIMER TO THE PROJECT

The timer creates a loose state if it takes too long to finish the maze.

1. Find it in the **Interface & Text** tab in your **Library**.

Interface & Text

2. Place it on the **User Interface** layer: from the **Appearance** tab in the **Inspector**.

Timer

00s:000ms

NOTES

This will allow the player to pick up the prize when they touch.

1.Open the Event Manager and create **New Event**
2. Do this by saying: "When my player touches the prize, the prize should set its position to the player"

PICK UP THE PRIZE

When

Player

Sensing

In Touching Object

Prize

Do

Prize

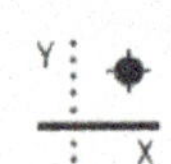

Position

Set Position For Object

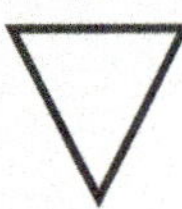
Player

ZAP PLAYER WHEN TOUCHING OBSTACLE

This will make the player "zap" and appear back at the start each time it touches an obstacle

OBSTACLE ZAP PLAYER

When

Player

Sensing

In Touching Object

Any from group Obstacle

Do

Player

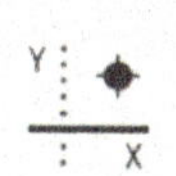

Position

Set Position To Object

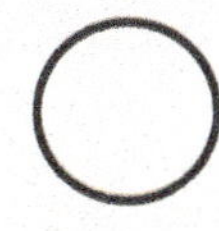
Home

Player

Impact Particle Effect

Run Effect

13 WIN AND STOP TIMER WHEN PRIZE IS BACK HOME

This will make the player "zap" and appear back at the start each time it touches an obstacle

WIN MOMENT

When	 Prize	 Sensing	 Is Touching Object	 Home
Do	 Prize	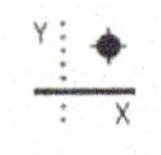 Position	 Set Position To Object	 Home
	 Timer	 Timer Label	 Set Active	 No
	 System	 Global	 Set Background Color	 Color

MAKE GAME HARDER

This will allow the player to pick up the prize when they touch

1. Do this by switching **ON Physics** in your **PLAYER'S control-pad** rom the **Behavior** settings in the **Inspector**.

  Physics 

TURN & TALK DISCUSSION

As a group or with your partner to answer the following questions.

- In what way does physics act to make it more difficult to control the character?
- Which step was the most challenging to build?
-Brainstorm at least one more item, behavior, object, or obstacle you could add to the maze game to make it more fun.

NOTES

COMPUTING CONCEPTS IN THIS PROJECT	
- Classes (obstacles) - Conditional Statements - Adding multiple consequences to conditional statements "+" - Solids vs Non-solids - Timer - Win moment	- Origin points (home base) - Cartesian location - Physics and Momentum - Setting Backgrounds - Playing Effects via conditional Events - Game Theory: Player / Prize dynamic.

BEHAVIORS & EFFECTS IN THIS PROJECT		
Stay in frame (PLAYER)	**Control pad** (PLAYER)	**Impact Particle** (PLAYER)

CONCLUSIONS

Stop
Watch

Stopwatch
Level: Intermediate

In this project, we'll make a stopwatch. This project uses original objects to represent seconds and milliseconds, and give the user the ability to start, stop and restart the watch.

STEPS TO BUILD

1. Add a SECOND HAND object, name it & make it non-solid
2. Add a SEC-PIVOT object, name it & make it non-solid
3. Give SEC-PIVOT "join" and "rotate" Behaviors
4. Create the "Pivot Class" & add your SEC-PIVOT object
5. Copy your SEC-PIVOT object and name is "MIL-PIVOT"
6. Add a MILLISECOND object, name it & make it non-solid
7. Connect SEC-PIVOT to SECOND object and set rotation
8. Connect MIL-PIVOT to MILLISEC-OND HAND object and set rotation
9. Add a START "text box" and Name it START
10. Add a STOP "text box" and Name it STOP
11. Add a RESTART "text box" and Name it RESTART
12. Event#1: START THE CLOCK WHEN "START" IS TOUCHED
13. Event#2: STOP THE CLOCK WHEN "STOP" IS TOUCHED
14. Event#3: RESET THE CLOCK WHEN "RESET" IS TOUCHED
15. Add a Background and any round object you want.
16. Add the 12 - 3 - 6 & 9 numbers and position them

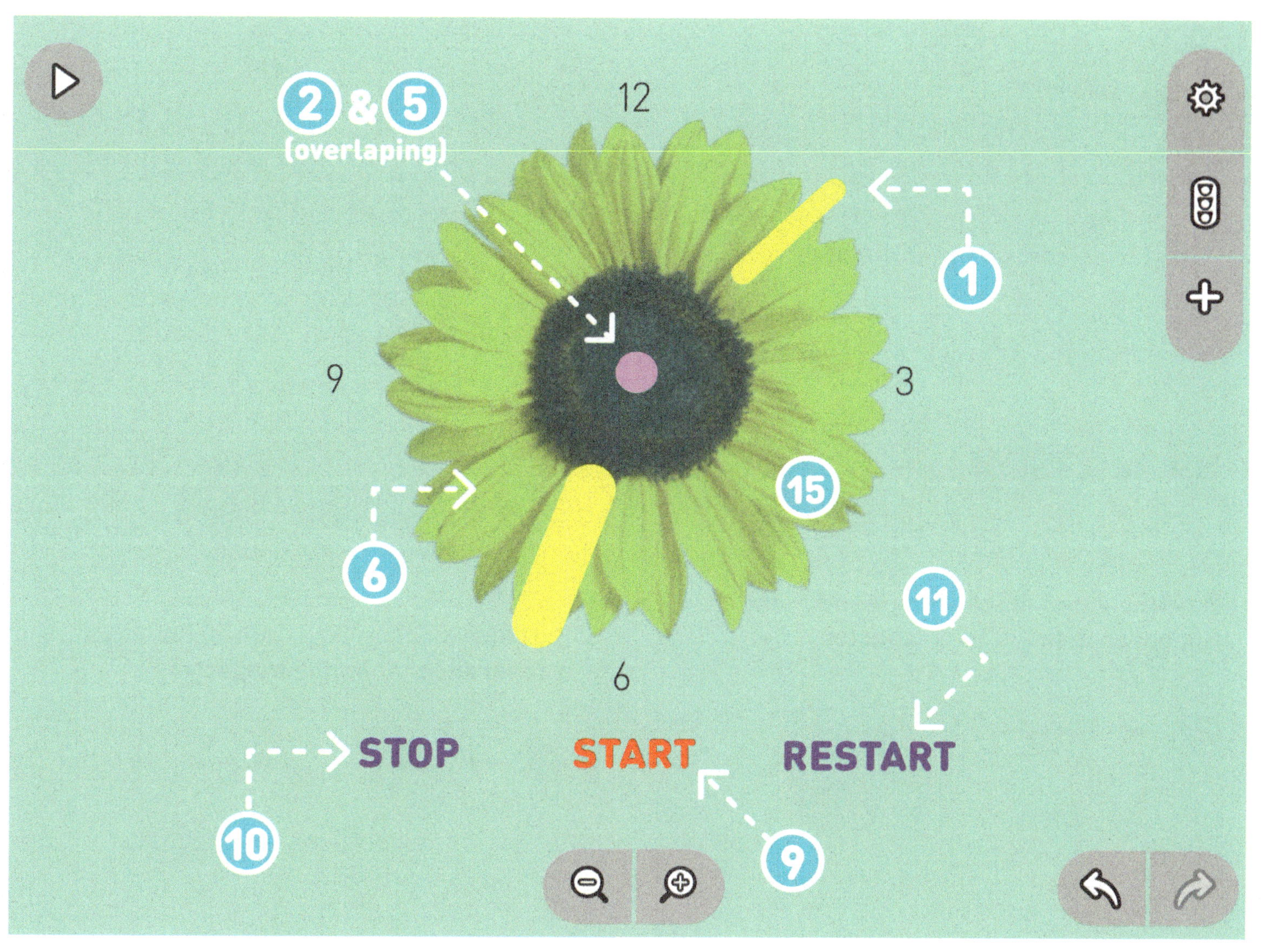
2 & 5
(overlaping)
12
1
9
3
15
6
11
6
STOP
START
RESTART
10
9

ADD A SECOND HAND OBJECT, NAME IT & MAKE IT NON-SOLID

This will be the object that marks the seconds on your stopwatch

1. Add it from the **Artwork** tab in the **Library.**

2. Name it and make it **non-solid** in the **Appearance** tab in the **Inspector**.

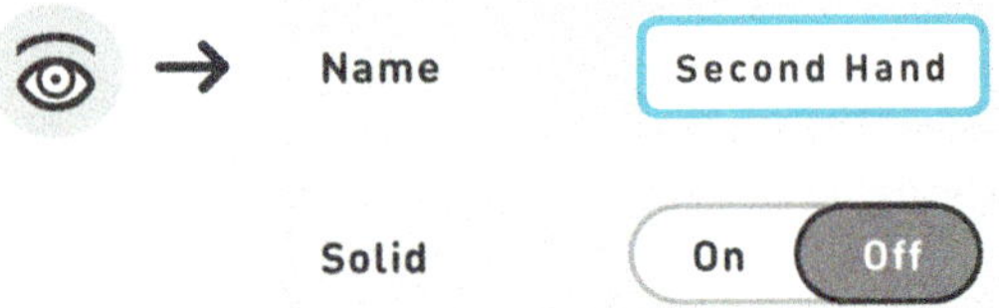

ADD A SEC-PIVOT OBJECT, NAME IT AND MAKE IT NON-SOLID

This will be the anchor point in the center that will rotate your second hand

1. Add it from the **Artwork** tab in the **Library.**

2. Name it and make it **non-solid** in the **Appearance** tab in the **Inspector**.

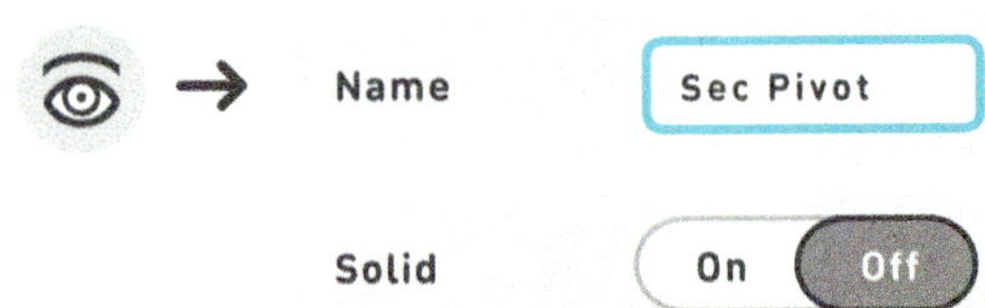

GIVE THE SEC-PIVOT "JOIN" & "ROTATE" BEHAVIORS

These will make the anchor point connect to and rotate the second hand

1. Drag the 2 behaviors to the objects from the **Behavior Tab** in the **Inspector**.

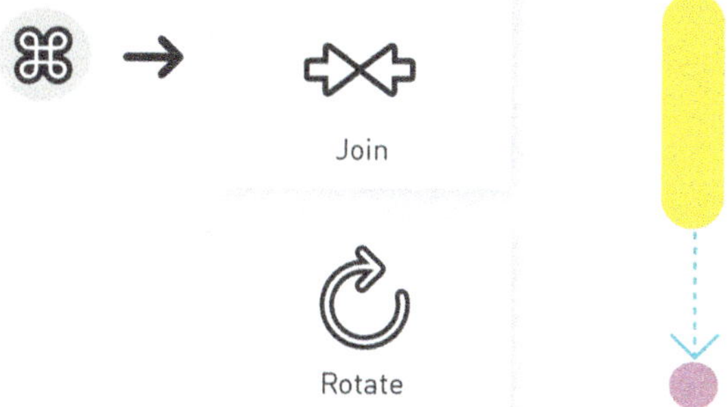

CREATE THE "PIVOT CLASS" & ADD YOUR SEC-PIVOT OBJECT

By making this a class, we can add objects to this class and they will inherit the same behaviors and appearances. All objects in this class will act and look the same way

1. Do this by selecting it, then taping **Create New Class** in the **Bucket icon** at the bottom of the **Inspector**.

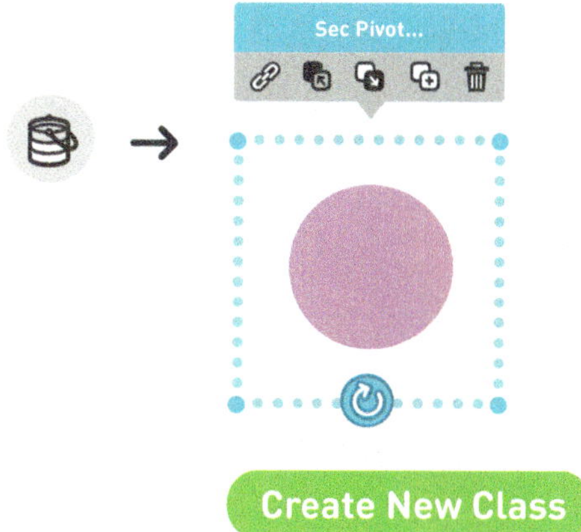

COPY THE SEC-PIVOT OBJECT & NAME IS "MIL-PIVOT"

We will use this one to rotate our millisecond hand

1. Copy it by taping the copy icon on the object's tooltip.

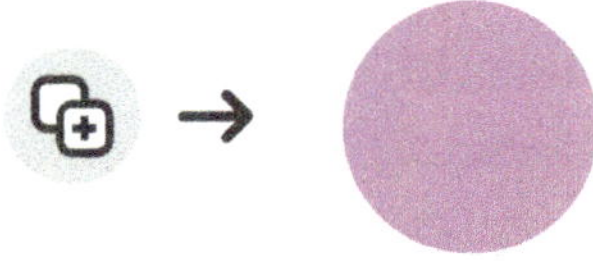

2. Name it in the **Appearance** tab in the **Inspector**.

ADD A MILLISECOND HAND OBJECT AND NAME IT & MAKE IT NON-SOLID

This will be the object that marks the milliseconds on your stopwatch

1. Add it from the **Artwork** tab in the **Library.**

2. Name it and make it **non-solid** in the **Appearance** tab in the **Inspector**.

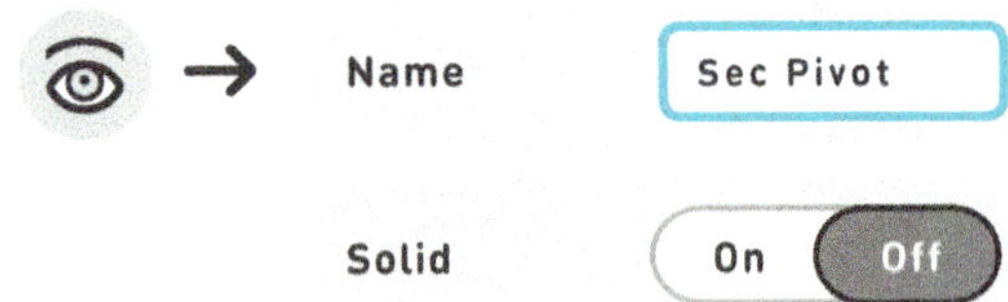

CONNECT THE SEC-PIVOT TO THE SECOND HAND OBJECT & SET ROTATION

Connect the anchor point to the second hand and give the correct rotation

1. Select **SEC-PIVOT** and join it to **SECOND HAND** from the **Behavior** tab in the **Inspector** under **join**.

2. Also set the rotation to 1rpm and toggle active to **OFF** from the **Behavior** tab in the **Inspector**.

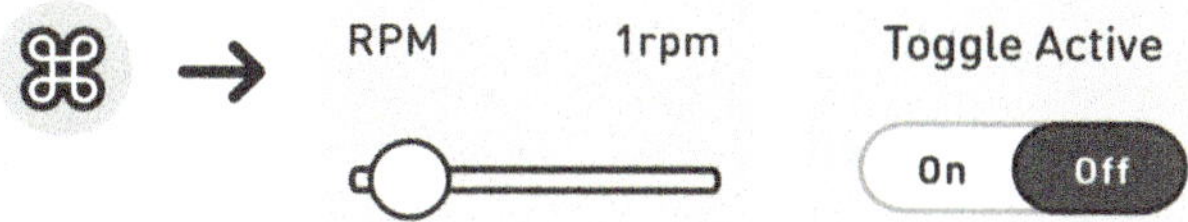

3. Change the Direction to **Clockwise**.

CONNECT YOUR MIL-PIVOT TO YOUR MILLISECOND HAND OBJECT

Connect the anchor point to the millisecond hand and give the correct rotation.

1. Select it and join it to **MILLISECOND** from the **Behavior** tab in the **Inspector**.

2. Also set the rotation to 60rpmwv and non active on start from the **Behavior** tab in the **Inspector**.

3. Change the Direction to **Clockwise**.

EXPERIMENT

Select the **SEC** and MIlli anchors and toggle **Active** to **ON** in the **Behaviors** tab under **join**. Play your project to see what happens. (Don't forget to toggle **Active** to **OFF** after the experiment!)

TRY THIS

1. Name the anchor that is moving faster. Could you create a stopwatch that shows the hour in Ready? Why or why not?
2. When you press play, 2 repetitive motions occur. With your partner, brainstorm ways that you could make the following concepts with Ready:
   - **A Seesaw**
   - **Wheels of a Car**
   - **An object moving down a slide**

How are these concepts related to the Stopwatch as shown here?

ADD A START "TEXT BOX" AND NAME IT START

You will use this to start the rotation of your pivot class

1. Drag it to your canvas from the **Interface & Text** tab in your **Library**.

START

2. Name it in the **Appearance** tab in the **Inspector**.

ADD A STOP "TEXT BOX" AND NAME IT STOP

You will use this to stop the rotation of your pivot class

1. Drag it to your canvas from the **Interface & Text** tab in your **Library**.

STOP

2. Name it in the **Appearance** tab in the **Inspector**.

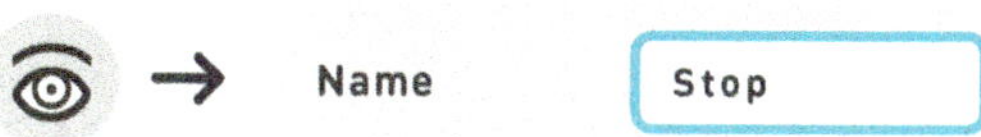

NOTES

ADD A RESTART "TEXT BOX" AND NAME IT RESTART

You will use this to restart your stopwatch

1. Drag it to your canvas from the **Interface & Text** tab in your **Library**.

RESTART

2. Name it in the **Appearance** tab in the **Inspector**.

Name Stop

EVENT #1 TO: START THE CLOCK WHEN "START" IS TOUCHED

This starts the rotation of the clock whenever the text "START" is tapped

1.Open the Event Manager and create **New Event.**
2. Do this by saying: "When start is touched rotate the pivot class".

 → 

START

When

Start

Sensing

Touch Down

Do

All class PIVOT

Rotate

Set Active

Yes

EVENT #2: STOP THE CLOCK WHEN "STOP" IS TOUCHED

This stops the rotation of the clock whenever the text "STOP" is tapped.

1. Open the Event Manager and create **New Event.**
2. Do this by saying: "When stop is touched, stop the rotation of the pivot class"

STOP

When	Stop	Sensing	Touch Down	
Do	 All class PIVOT	 Rotate	Set Active	 No

EVENT #3: RESET THE CLOCK WHEN "RESET" IS TOUCHED

This resets the clock whenever the text "RESTART" is tapped.

1. Open the Event Manager and create **New Event.**
2. Do this by saying: "When reset is touched, the system should reset".

RESET

When	RESET	Sensing	Touch Down
Do	System	System	Restart Scene

NOTES

SET UP THE WATCH WITH A PROJECT BACKGROUND

Create the look of a stopwatch and add a personal style

1. Add a background from the **Background** tab in the **Library**.

2. Add a round watchface from the **Artwork** tab in the **Library** and place it in the **background layer** from the appearance tab in the inspector.

3. Position your anchor points in the middle of the watch face, and place your hands so that they are pointing straight up in the center of the anchor points.

ADD THE 12 - 3 - 6 & 9 NUMBERS AND POSITION THEM

Numbers serve as guides for time. Decorate your project with any other ideas that come to mind.

1. Drag it to your canvas from the **Interface & Text** tab in your **Library**.

2. Lay them out in the correct positions.

TURN & TALK DISCUSSION

As a group or with your partner to answer the following questions.

As a group or with your partner, to answer the following questions.
Review the steps to build and identify the two challenging steps.

Write down how these steps work within Ready. Use details and refer back to the step-by-step directions.

Explain why these steps are difficult, and why they are important to the function of the project.

COMPUTING CONCEPTS IN THIS PROJECT	
- Classes (obstacles) - Conditional Statements - Solids vs Non-solids	- "Button" as Trigger - Active / Inactive on start - Setting Backgrounds
BEHAVIORS & EFFECTS IN THIS PROJECT	
Join (Anchor)	**Rotation** (Anchor)

CONCLUSIONS

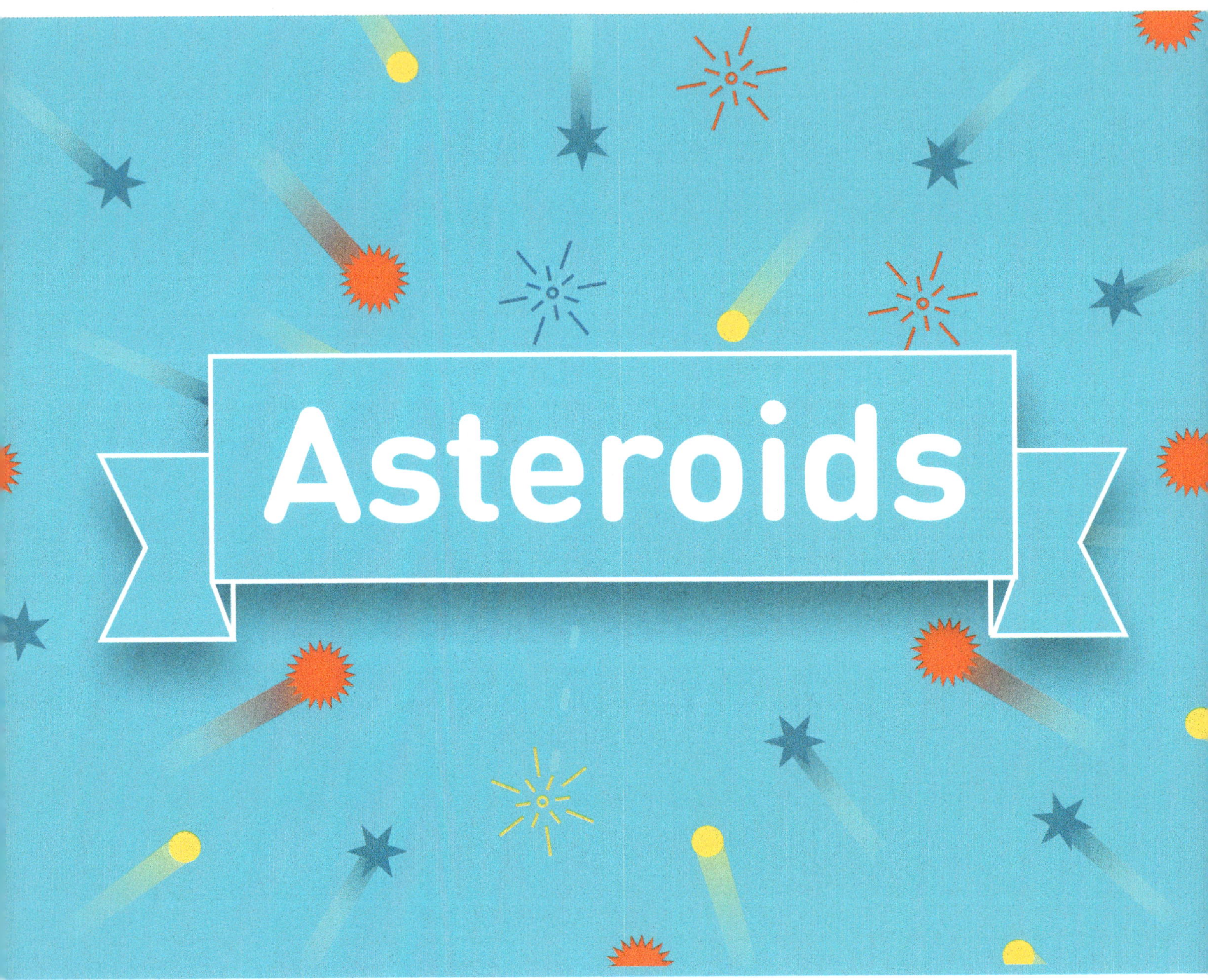
Asteroids

Asteroids

Level: Begginer

In Asteroids, the **PLAYER** controls a **SPACESHIP** in the center of the screen, avoiding incoming **asteroids**. The **PLAYER** launches missiles to destroy incoming **ASTEROIDS**, before the asteroids can destroy the ship. When the **SHIP** is destroyed, the game ends.

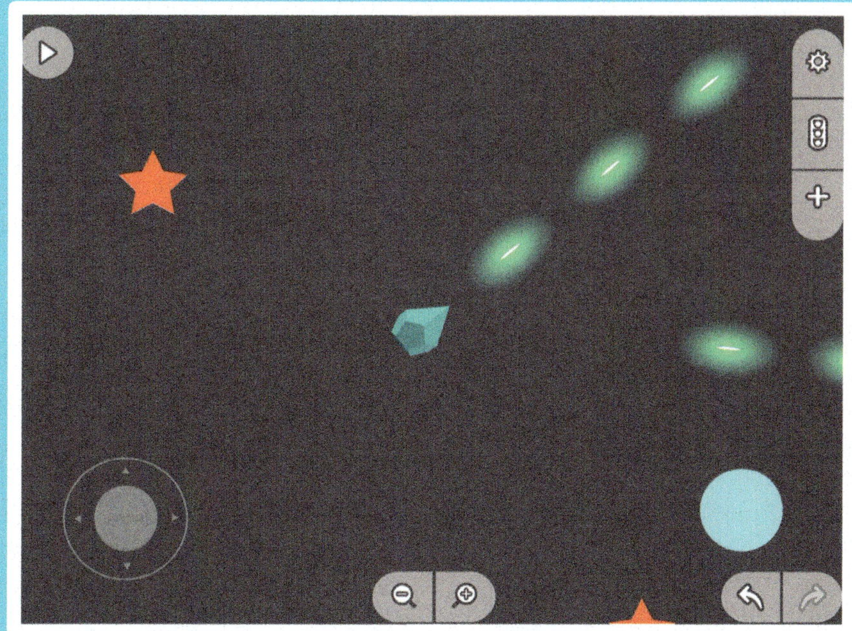

STEPS TO BUILD

1. Add PLAYER
2. Add CLONER
3. Add CENTERPOINT
4. Give CENTERPOINT object "Hinge" Behavior
5. Event #1: Camera & CENTERPOINT follow PLAYER
6. Give PLAYER "Control pad" Behavior.
7. Turn on "General Physics" for PLAYER
8. Add ASTEROID object, give it "Move Towards" Behavior
9. Create & assign it to the "Asteroid Class"
10. Add 2 arched lines to lock master ASTEROID
11. Add laser object. Give it the "Impact" Effect
12. Create & assign it to the "Laser Class"
13. Add LAUNCH object to use as a button
14. Event #2: Move Lasers
15. Event #3: Shoot lasers when LAUNCH is pressed
16. Event #4: Remove old laser clones
17. Event #5: Clone ASTEROID
18. Event #6: Destroy ASTEROID when collided with laser
19. Event #7: PLAYER lose when touching ASTEROID

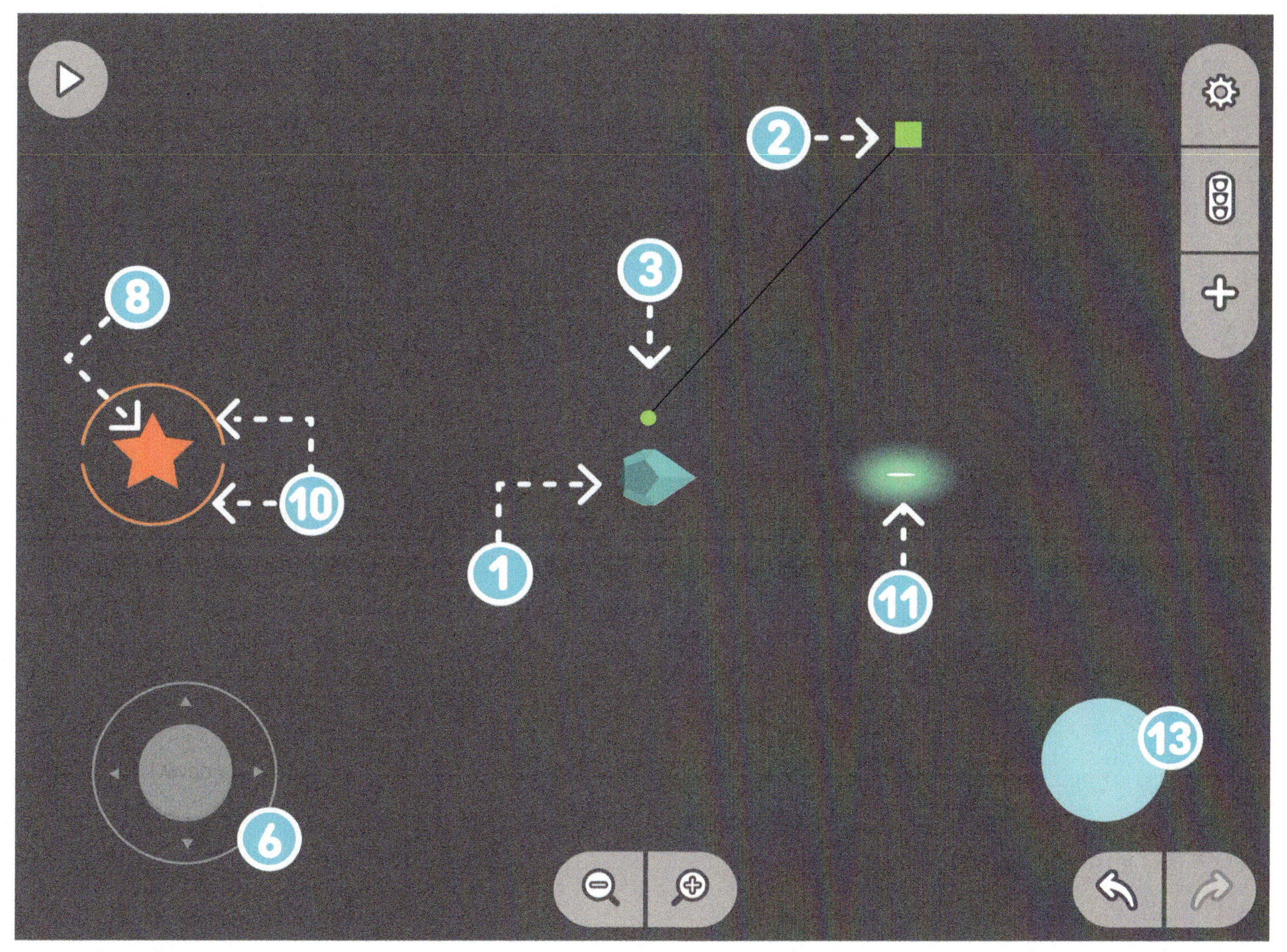

2
3
8
10
1
11
13
6

ADD PLAYER, NAME IT & MAKE IT NON SOLID

This is the spaceship

1. From **Library / Artwork**: Add ship

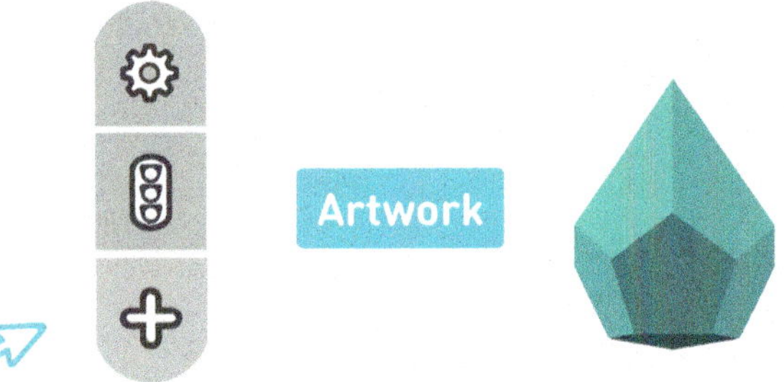

2. From **Inspector / Appearance**: Name ship and make it "non-solid"

ADD A CLONER OBJECT & MAKE IT NON SOLID

This object orbits the spaceship cloning asteroids

1. Add it from the **Basic shapes** tab in the **Library**.

2. From **Inspector / Appearance**: Name it and make it "non-solid"

ADD A CENTERPOINT OBJECT & MAKE IT NON SOLID

This serves as the centerpoint that rotates your cloner object

Add it from the **Basic shapes** tab in the **Library**.

2. From **Inspector / Appearance**:
Name it and make it "non-solid"

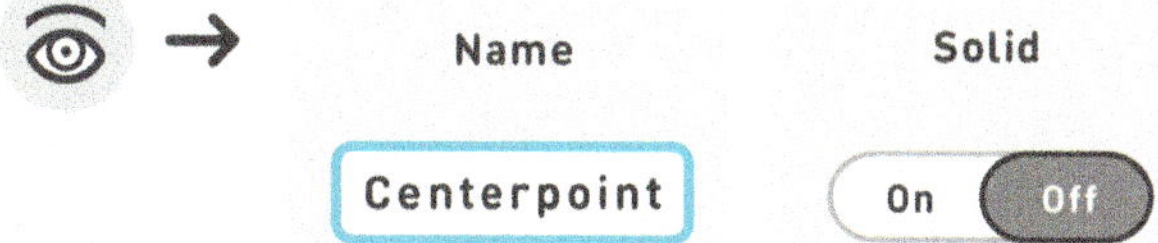

3. Make it smaller than the player.
Set it behind the ship from the tooltip.

NOTES

TURN ON "GENERAL PHYSICS" ON PLAYER AND ADD DRAG

This allows the player to move. It can be fine-tuned later

1. From Physics: Switch **On** Physics and **Off** Gravity.

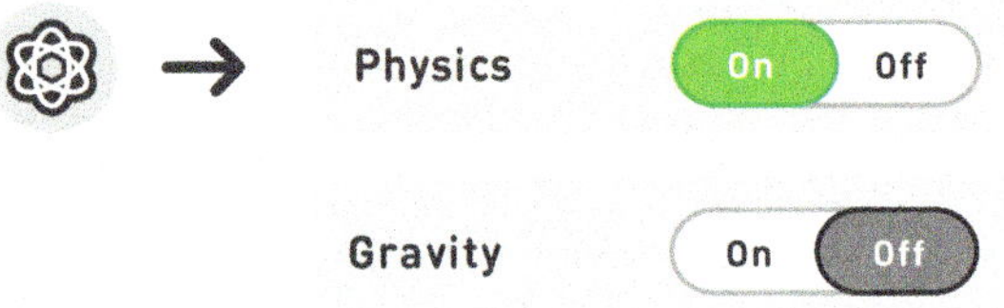

2. Set the **Drag** to 6%

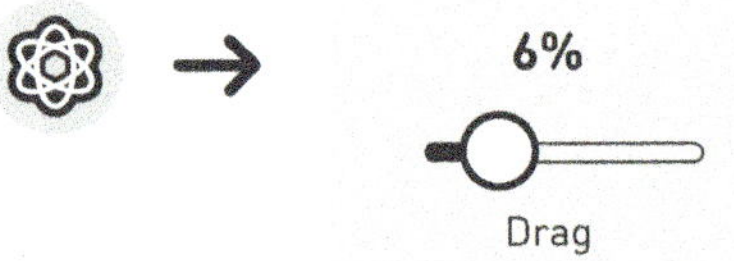

TURN & TALK ANTICIPATE

As a group or with your partner to answer the following questions.

Now you have some objects of the game on your canvas. Notice that whenever you move the spaceship, everything is still in the center.

Identify the parts as Cloner Object, Centerpoint, and Spaceship as they're moving. Turn on the "Show Joint at runtime" from behaviors of centerpoint object to see more clearly.

Make a list of things that need to change or items that must be added to the current project in order to make the final game as you understand it.

Explain to your partner what you think the rotating items will be used for?

ADD AN ASTEROID & GIVE IT MOVE TOWARDS BEHAVIOR

This generates the objects moving towards the ship to avoid or destroy

1. Add it from the **Artwork** tab in the **Library**.

2. Add the **Move Towards** Behavior and set the **Object** to **Player** and speed to 1.5 m/s.

3. Make the **Active zone** 25m and switch **ON** the physics of that **Move Towards**.

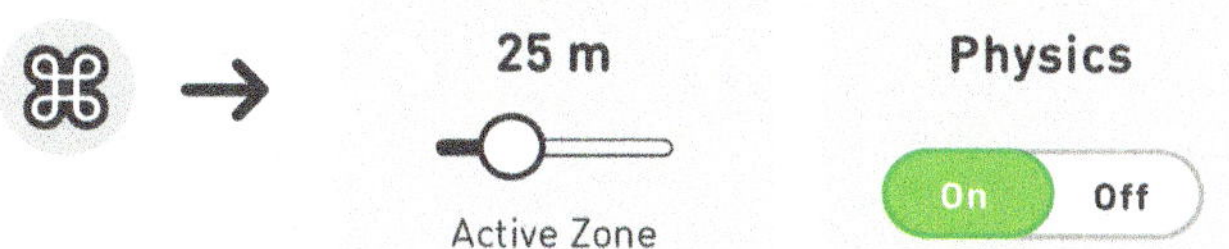

CREATE & ASSIGN IT TO THE "ASTEROID CLASS"

This activates the ability to send instructions to all the cloned asteroids

1. Set Class: Select the asteroid object, and tap **Create New Class** in the **Bucket icon** at the bottom of the **Inspector**.

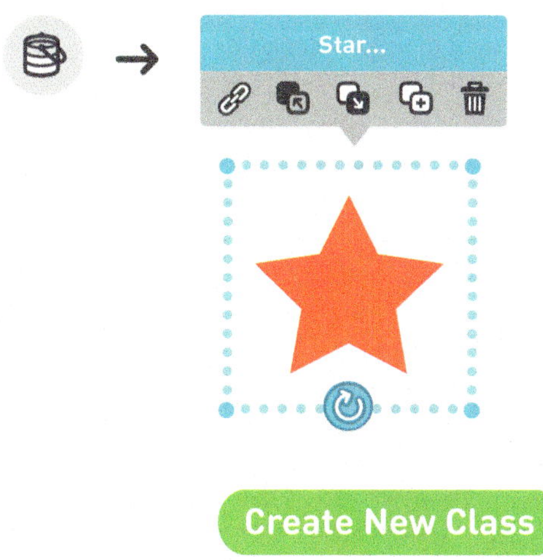

ADD 2 ARCHED LINES & LOCK THE MASTER ASTEROID

This keeps the master asteroid offscreen so it can be cloned and never destroyed

1. From **Library:** Get the arched lines.

2. Hide them from event manager.

3. Zoom out to move the asteroid and enclose it with the two arches.

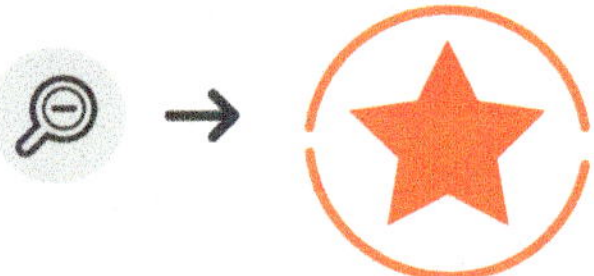

4. From **Appearance**: Set their opacity to 0%.

ADD A LASER OBJECT & GIVE IT "IMPACT EFFECT"

The spaceship launches lasers and runs the effect when asteroids are hit

1. Get it from the **Library**.

2. From **Effects**:
Add the **Impact Effect**.

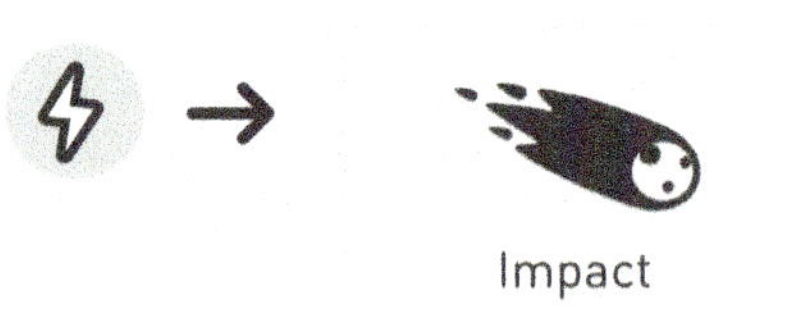

CREATE & ASSIGN IT TO THE "LASER CLASS"

This enables giving instructions to all the clones

1. Select object, then tap **Create New Class** in the **Bucket icon** at the bottom of the **Inspector**.

TURN & TALK DISCUSSION

As a group or with your partner to answer the following questions.

- In this game, asteroids will come towards the spaceship in multiple directs, so the spaceship must do two things.
- Discuss what those two actions are with your partner, as well as how the user will do them.
- Brainstorm 3 different ways that the user could win this game.

ADD A LAUNCH OBJECT & PLACE IT ON THE USER INTERFACE LAYER

This acts as a button to launch lasers

1. Add it from the **Basic Shapes** tab in the **Library.**

Basic Shapes

2. From **Inspector / Appearance**: Name it and place it on the **User interface** layer.

Layer User Interface

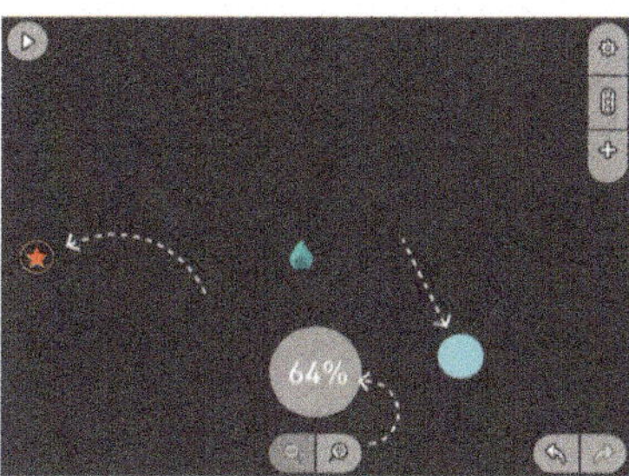

14 EVENT #2: MOVE LASERS

The lasers to move forward whenever it appears on screen

1. Open the Event Manager and create **New Event**
2. Do this by saying: "When anything in laser class is seen move it forward 5 m/s".

MOVE BULLETS

When	 Any in Laser Class	 Sensing	 Seen	 Yes
Do	 Affected object from class Bullet	Movement	Move Forward Over Time	 5 m/s

EVENT #3: SHOOT LASERS WHEN LAUNCH PRESSED

Ther spaceship clones lasers when the launch button is tapped

SHOOT BUTTON

When	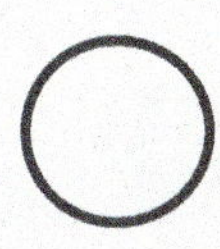 Launch	 Sensing	 Touch Down	
Do	 Player	 Clone	 Clone Object	 Laser
	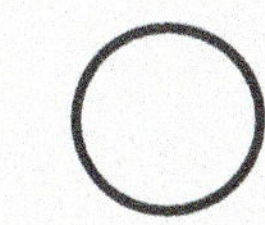 Bordered Circle	 Sound	 Play Sound	 Shoot

EVENT #4: REMOVE OLD LASER CLONES

To save memory, remove laser clones after a certain time

1.Open the Event Manager and create **New Event.**
2. Do this by saying: "When anything in laser class existed longer than 4s remove it".

DESTROY BULLETS

When

Any in Laser Class

Runtime

Existed Longer Than

4

Do

Affected object from Laser Class

Clone

Remove Clone

EVENT #5: CLONE ASTEROID EVERY 2 SECONDS

Tell cloner object to clone an asteroid every 2 or 3 seconds

1.Open the Event Manager and create **New Event**
2. Do this by saying: "When the system counts every 3 seconds,cloner make another asteroid"

CLONE ASTEROIDS

When	 System	 Runtime	 Repeat Every	 3
Do	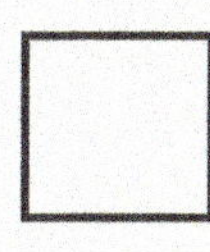 Cloner	 Clone	 Clone Object	 Star

EVENT #6: DESTROY ASTEROID WHEN COLLIDED WITH LASER

Tell anything in the "asteroid class" to disappear when it's touched by a laser

DESTROY ASTEROID *Change "bullet" to "laser, throughout

When	Any in Laser Class	Sensing	Is Touching Object	Any from group Asteroid
Do	Affected object from class Asteroid	Clone	Remove Clone	
	Affected object from Laser Class	Sound	Play Sound	Hit1
	Affected object from Laser Class	IMPACT Particle Effect	Run Effect	

EVENT #7: PLAYER LOSE WHEN TOUCHING ASTEROID

Let's create a loose state when an asteroid touches our spaceship

LOSE MOMENT

When	 Any in class Asteroid	 Sensing	 In Touching Object	 Player
Do	 System	 Global	 Set Background Color	 Color
	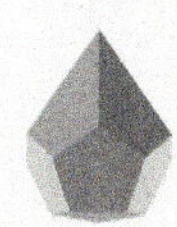 Player	 Appearance	 Set Hidden	 Yes

COMPUTING CONCEPTS IN THIS PROJECT

- Classes
- Conditional Statements
- Adding multiple consequences to conditional statements "+"
- Solids vs Non-solids
- Cloning
- Using the Camera
- User Interface
- Lose moment
- Cartesian location
- Physics and Momentum
- Setting Backgrounds
- Playing Effects via conditional Events
- Game Theory: Object offscreen

BEHAVIORS & EFFECTS IN THIS PROJECT

MoveTowards	Control pad	Impact Effect	Hinge

CONCLUSIONS

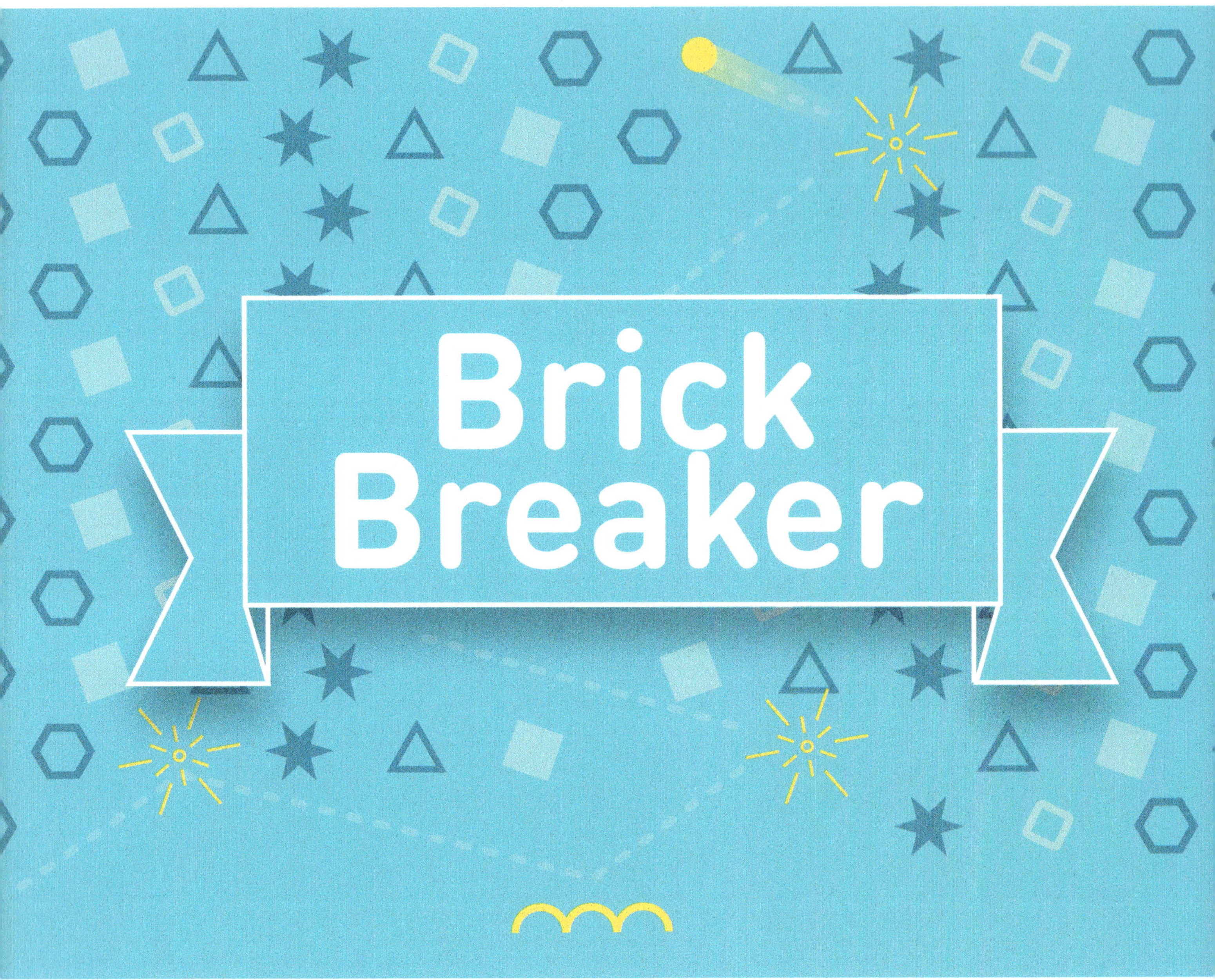
Brick
Breaker

Brick Breaker

Level: Intermediate

In this game, the player moves a **PADDLE** from side-to-side to hit a **BALL**. The game's objective is to eliminate all of the **BRICKS** at the top of the screen by hitting them with the **BALL**. But, if the ball hits the bottom **ENCLOSURE**, the player loses and the game ends! To win the game, all the **BRICKS** must be eliminated.

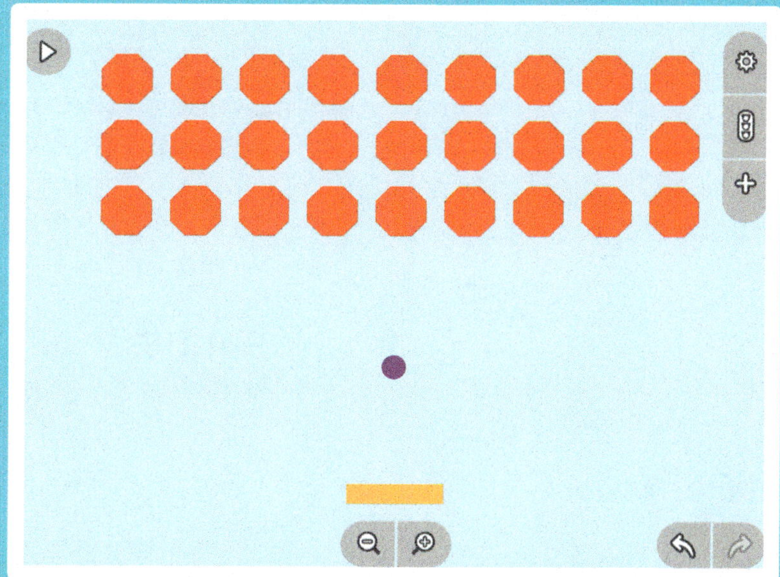

STEPS TO BUILD

1. Add BALL
2. Add a RECTANGLE to create an ENCLOSURE
3. Set up ENCLOSURE
4. Give BALL Behaviors and Effects
5. Add PADDLE
6. Give PADDLE Behaviors
7. Add a BRICK
8. Create the "BRICK class" and copy
9. Event #1: Remove BRICK when hit by BALL
10. Event #2: Restart scene when BALL touches "BAD"
11. BONUS: Make game harder by adjusting object speeds.

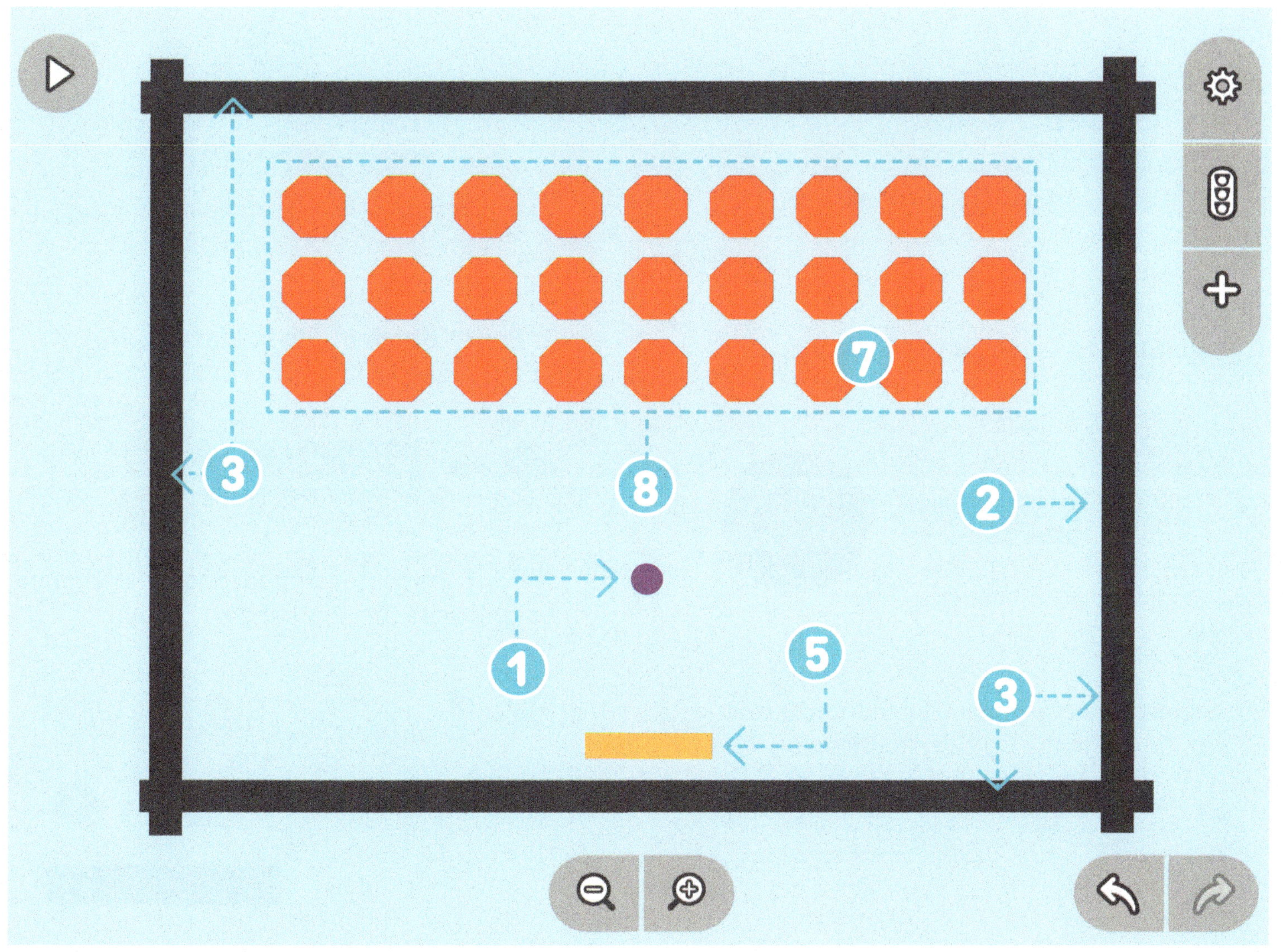

1
2
3
3
5
7
8

ADD BALL

The ball bounces between the bricks (top), and paddle (bottom).

1. From **Shapes** tab in **Library**: add circle.

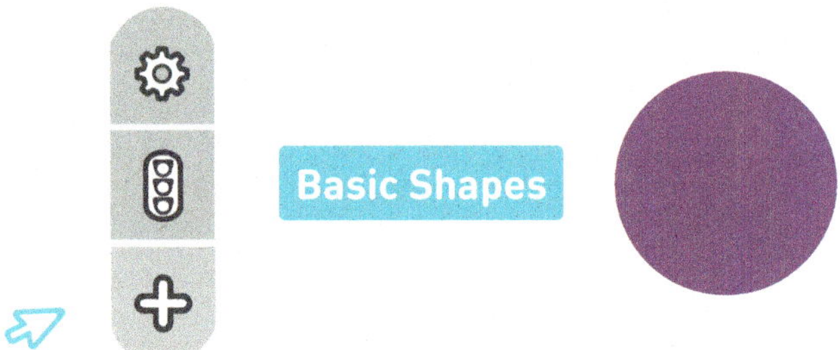

2. From inspector appearance tab: Name BALL and Change Collider to **Circular**.

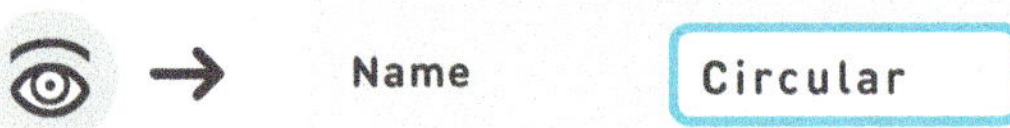

ADD A RECTANGLE FOR ENCLOSURE

Create a game space by making an enclosure to contain the ball

1. From "**Shapes**" tab in **Library**: add rectangle

2. From inspector **Appearance** tab: change height to be 5m High and tint it black.

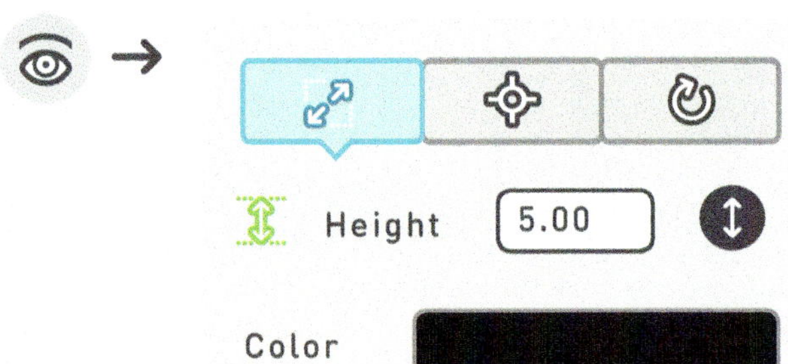

SET UP ENCLOSURE

Define the game space by placing enclosures at the edges of the canvas.

1. Zoom out twice.

2. From tooltip: Duplicate enclosure three times for a total of 4 rectangles.

3. From inspector appearance tab: Rotate two of the rectangles so 2 are horizontal and 2 are vertical and arrange these 4 rectangles into a box.

4. From inspector appearance tab: Name the bottom enclosure **BAD**.

  Name Bad

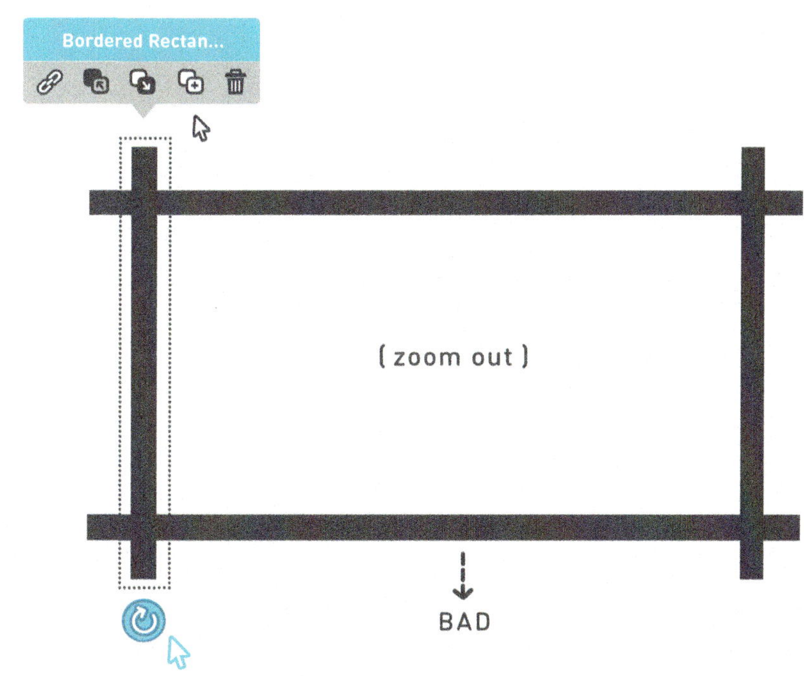

GIVE BALL BEHAVIORS AND EFFECTS

Give a movement to your ball so that it can move within the enclosure

1. Add the **Bullet** behavior and change the **Bullet** behavior by setting the angle to 300 degrees.

2. Change the **Bullet** behavior speed to approximately 3 m/s and toggle its **Bounce** to **ON**.

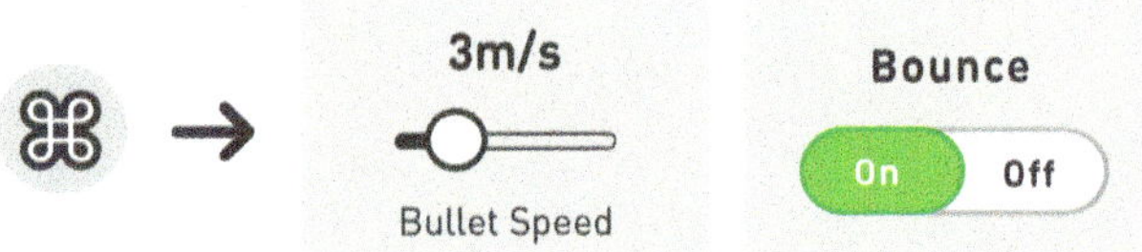

2. From **Effects**: Add the **Impact** effect.

ADD PADDLE

Create an item that can be used to hit the ball

1. From **Library**: Add rectangle

2. From **Appearance**: Name rectangle and rotate to **90** degrees.

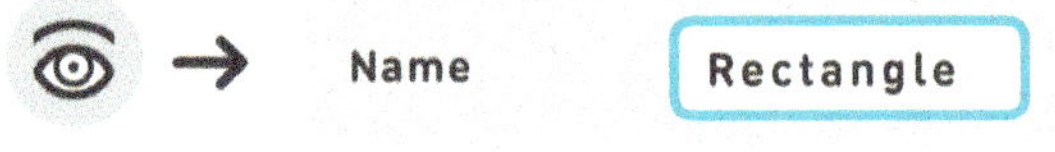

3. Resize **PADDLE** width to approixmately same size as one square on the canvas grid.

6 GIVE PADDLE BEHAVIORS

Give paddle behaviors and effects to move from side to side and deflect the ball, as it bounces from the bricks on top towards the bottom enclosure

1. From **Behaviors**: Add the **Control Pad** to your paddle. Change its directions to **Left & Right**.

2. Place **PADDLE** towards bottom of enclosure, so that it almost touches **BAD** enclosure object.

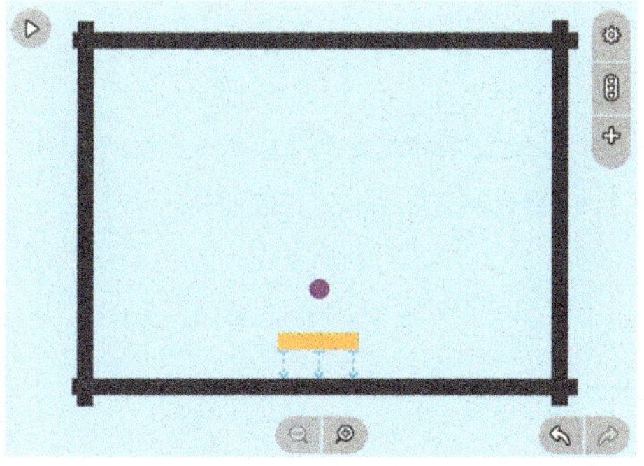

EXPERIMENT

Place your paddle about 2 square units away from the bottom and play your project.

TRY THIS

1. What happens when the ball gets underneath the paddle?
2. What happens when you copy the ball a few times and play the project again?
3. What happens if you turn physics "On" from the **Behaviors** tab on the control pad of your paddle?

NOTES

ADD BRICK

Create an object along the top of the game space for the BALL to hit and destroy

1. From **Library**: Add a brick object. Choose any image style.

2. From **Appearance**: Name object.

3. Change it's **Collider** to **Box** and toggle its **Show in Event Manager** to **OFF**.

CREATE THE "BRICK CLASS" AND COPY

Classes provide instructions to objects as a group instead of individuals. With a class, one event can apply to all the bricks on screen.

1. From **Classes**: Select **BRICK**. Select **Bucket Icon** from the bottom of the **Inspector** and **Create New Class**.

2. From the tool tip box: Duplicate original brick as many times as desired.Line bricks up in 2- 3 rows at the top of game space.

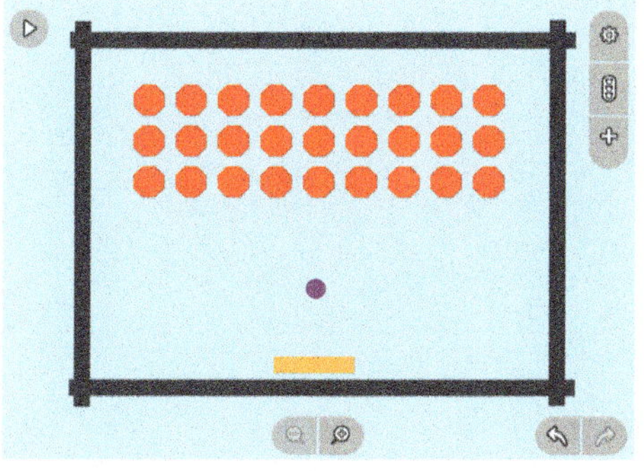

TURN & TALK ANTICIPATE

As a group or with your partner to answer the following questions.

Turn and talk with your partner to discuss the objective of the game and write it down.

Discuss what you think should happen if the ball hits the BRICKS, and write down the steps that would occur in detail..

Discuss what you think should happen if the ball hits the paddle and write down the steps that should occur. Then, write down the steps of what should happen if the ball hits the "BAD" enclosure.

EVENT #1: REMOVE BRICK WHEN HIT BY BALL

This will make the bricks disappear if they are hit by the ball.

REMOVE BRICK

When	Ball	Sensing	Collided With Object	Any from group Brick
Do	Affected object from class Brick	Appearence	Set Hidden	Yes
	Ball	IMPACT Particle Effect	Run Effect	
	Ball	Sound	Play Sound	Enter1

EVENT #2: RESTART SCENE WHEN BALL TOUCHES "BAD"

This restarts the game if the ball touches the "BAD" enclousure

1.Open the Event Manager and create **New Event**
2. Do this by saying: "When the ball hits the "BAD" enclosure, restart the game."

LOSE AND RESTART *Change the word "Puck" to "Ball" in the first box

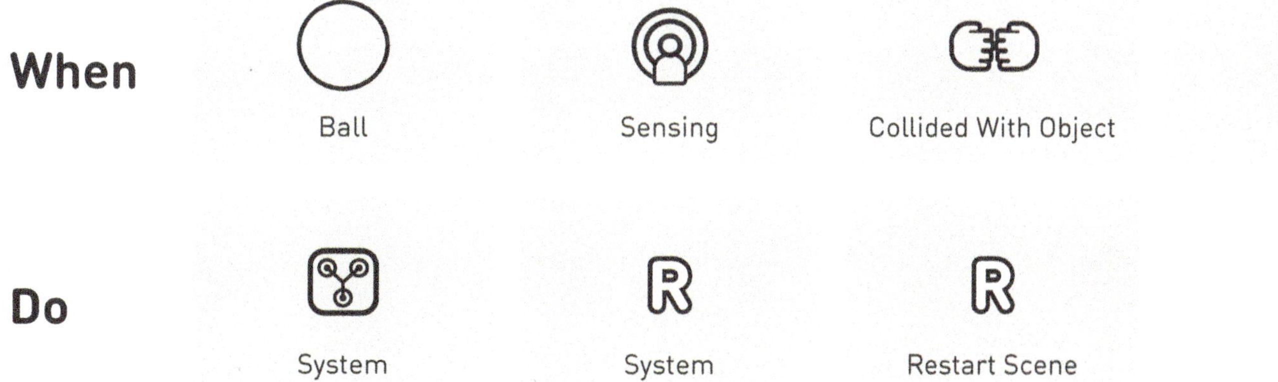

BONUS: MAKE YOUR GAME HARDER

Make game harder by adjusting object speeds

1. Experiment with the position and speed of the ball and paddle to make the game more challenging.

TURN & TALK DISCUSSION

As a group or with your partner to answer the following questions.

- Why didn't you need to make an event for the ball to move back up after hitting the paddle?
- Looking at the event manager, what is the difference between "Sensing" and "Collided With"?
- Does the project work the same if you change the BALL item? What if you pick a shape that isn't round? Why or why not?
- Refer back to your prediction about the steps that should occur when the ball hits the "BAD" enclosure. In what ways were your predictions accurate? What steps did you miss?

CONCLUSIONS

COMPUTING CONCEPTS IN THIS PROJECT

- Classes (Bricks)
- Conditional Statements
- Adding multiple consequences to conditional statements "+"
- Hiding object from Events
- Restarting your scen.
- Origin points (home base)
- Physics and Momentum
- Triggering Effects via conditional Events

BEHAVIORS & EFFECTS IN THIS PROJECT

Control pad (PLAYER)	**Impact Particle** (PLAYER)	**Control pad** (PLAYER)	**Impact Particle** (PLAYER)

READY MAKERS

CPSIA information can be obtained
at www.ICGtesting.com
Printed in the USA
BVOW10s2053051116
467042BV00003B/3/P